GREENHOUSE GARDENER

Alan Toogood

ARCO PUBLISHING, INC.
New York

Endpaper *A showy display of the foliage and flowers of both house and garden plants can be combined in the sheltered environment of a cool greenhouse.*

Facing title page *Located in a sunny corner of the garden, this barn-type greenhouse adds endless variety to the plants and crops that can be grown around the year.*

Right *Even in very limited space, a wide range of home produce can be grown: here, climbing green and dwarf snap beans, tomatoes, peppers, celery, eggplants and a pot of parsley are crowded together on one shelf.*

American Editor: Edwin F. Steffek

Published by Arco Publishing, Inc.
215 Park Avenue South, New York, N.Y. 10003

Copyright © 1985 Marshall Cavendish Limited

Library of Congress Cataloging In Publication Data

Toogood, Alan R.
    Greenhouse Gardener.

1. Greenhouse gardening. 2. Greenhouses. I. Title.
SB415.T67   1985   635.9'823   84–21650

ISBN 0-668-06410-2

Printed in Hong Kong

CONTENTS

INTRODUCTION

More and more nowadays, greenhouses form part of the garden scene. Besides helping you run your garden efficiently, greenhouse gardening is a hobby to be enjoyed all year round.

Greenhouse gardening has probably never been more popular than it is today and there have certainly never been more types and styles of greenhouse to choose from. There are greenhouses available to suit every pocket, all sizes of garden, and every type of plant, from the ever-popular tomato to decorative pot plants, orchids and cacti.

Why have a greenhouse?
There are several very good reasons why every gardener should have a greenhouse. Firstly, it enables you to carry on gardening all through the year, no matter what the weather may be doing. A far wider range of plants can be grown, but the choice does depend on the amount of artificial heat you are able to provide. Even without heat, though, a good range of tender plants, such as tomatoes, cucumbers and peppers, can still be grown out of season. Various fruits,

like tender grapes, will succeed, and in the winter and spring the cool greenhouse can protect pots of colorful bulbs, primroses and alpines, as well as useful crops of lettuce and other vegetables.

Of course, you will be able to raise all kinds of plants from seeds, instead of buying them from garden centers, which works out much cheaper. Examples are summer bedding plants for the garden, flowering pot plants, which can also be used in the home, and tender vegetables for planting in the garden. By raising your own plants from seeds you will be able to choose cultivars (varieties) from seed catalogs which really appeal to you, instead of relying on the limited selections found in most garden centers.

Greenhouse gardening is, of course, a hobby in itself, and many thousands of gardeners gain great pleasure simply from

A very wide range of fruits and vegetables can be grown in a greenhouse, and if artificial heat is provided many of these can be enjoyed out of season. Among the easiest fruits to grow are strawberries, and fruits can be harvested several weeks ahead of plants grown in the open.

growing plants under glass. It is safe to say that this form of gardening calls for greater skills and more attention to detail and plant care than outdoor gardening. A great deal of fun is involved in learning new skills, such as sowing seeds in trays, pricking out or transplanting seedlings, raising plants from cuttings, and controlling the growing conditions by shading, ventilating, damping down and providing the right heat.

It may sound as though all this is time consuming, with plants needing constant attention, but in fact many aspects, such as ventilation, heating and even watering, can be automated, so that it is possible to leave a greenhouse unattended for several days. And these days automation in the greenhouse need not be expensive.

Florists' flowers are very expensive today, but cut flowers for the home can be produced very economically if you have a greenhouse – and with very little or no artificial heat. Among the easiest and most popular are late-flowering chrysanthemums, perpetual-flowering carnations and freesias.

Conservatories

So far we have been discussing the traditional type of greenhouse, but there is great interest today in conservatories and lean-to greenhouses, which are erected against a house wall. They are used not only for growing plants but also as an extension of the home – an extra room which can be used for relaxation, entertaining and for leisure activities. What is more, these types of structure are more economical to heat, because they retain heat far better than a free-standing greenhouse.

Today there is no clear dividing line between a conservatory and a lean-to greenhouse – many of the latter are often termed conservatories. The true conservatory, which was popular in Victorian times, appears as an integral part of the house – not looking as though it has been added on at a later date. It should match the style of the house – in other words, an ultra-modern design would not look right with a Victorian house, and a Victorian design (which can still be obtained today) would look out of place on a modern house.

A conservatory, or a lean-to greenhouse, ideally should have access from the house and is an ideal place to display pot plants. The walls of the structure, especially the back wall, can be clothed with climbing plants or even with a grape vine. Permanent shrubby plants, like palms and oleanders, and maybe some citrus fruits, can be grown in a soil bed or in large ornamental containers and pots. Throughout the year the conservatory could be supplied with pot plants raised in the greenhouse.

A garden feature

A free-standing greenhouse is quite a dominant feature in the average-sized garden and so it needs to be of pleasing appearance if it is to be sited in the ornamental part of the garden. Fortunately there are many attractive designs available. But there are also "utility" greenhouses intended really for growing crops like tomatoes, cucumbers and other vegetables, and included here are polyethylene, walk-in tunnel houses, and other polyethylene structures. The best place for these is in a vegetable garden, ideally screened from the ornamental part. It really pays to have a good look around greenhouse centers before buying, to see what is available. There are quite a few points to consider – not only appearance – and these are discussed in Chapter One.

If a greenhouse is to be sited in an ornamental part of the garden it should be of attractive design and be constructed of materials which blend in with or complement the surroundings. Utility type houses are best hidden from view in the vegetable garden.

CHAPTER 1
CHOOSING A GREENHOUSE

A greenhouse is likely to be the most expensive purchase you will make for your garden, so consider the various greenhouses available, and what their strong and weak points are, before you make your choice.

A greenhouse should be chosen with care, for, like a house, it is a long-term investment. You should first decide what the greenhouse is to be used for and then choose a suitable type. For instance, if you intend growing plants mainly at ground level, such as tomatoes out of season, chrysanthemums in autumn, and salad crops and lettuce during the winter, then choose a model which is glazed to the ground on all sides, to ensure maximum light.

However, if you intend to go in mainly for pot plants, which can also include more specialist subjects like orchids, alpines and cacti, then the ideal greenhouse would have solid sides and ends to bench height, which is approximately 3ft (1m). Generally the solid sides are formed of timber, but it is also possible to have brick sides and ends. This type of greenhouse retains heat much better than one glazed to ground level and is therefore more economical to heat. This is an important consideration, especially if your garden is in a cold area.

Or you could compromise and have a greenhouse glazed to the ground on one side, where you could have a soil border for growing tomatoes and other crops, with the other three sides being solid to bench height, where pot plants can be grown.

Consider the appearance
As mentioned previously, if the greenhouse is to be sited in the ornamental part of the garden it needs to look good and, as far as possible, blend in with the surroundings. Greenhouses with a framework of western red cedar always look attractive and aluminum houses with an anodized bronze finish blend in beautifully with the garden. White-painted timber or raw aluminum do not blend in so well, although these materials do look good when used for lean-to greenhouses and conservatories.

Where to buy
Having decided on the basic type, start looking around to see what models are available. There are many greenhouse makers throughout the country and many garden centers also have greenhouse display sites. Some of the large chain stores sell greenhouses and you can also buy direct from manufacturers. The latter often advertise in gardening magazines and national newspapers and it is a good idea to send for their catalogs and price lists.

What size?
The best advice here is to buy the largest you can afford – provided it does not completely dominate the garden. There are

Below left *This is the traditional even-span greenhouse with solid sides to bench height. Such a house is ideal for the cultivation of pot plants, as well as more specialist plants like orchids, alpines and cacti.*

Below right *The traditionally shaped greenhouse can also be obtained with glass virtually to the ground, and is ideal if you intend growing plants such as tomatoes, chrysanthemums and winter salad crops, mainly at ground level. Benches can also be installed on which to grow pot plants.*

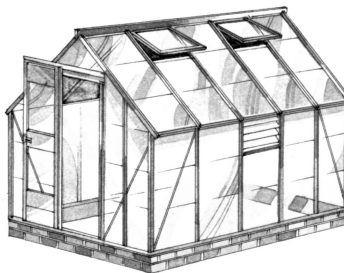

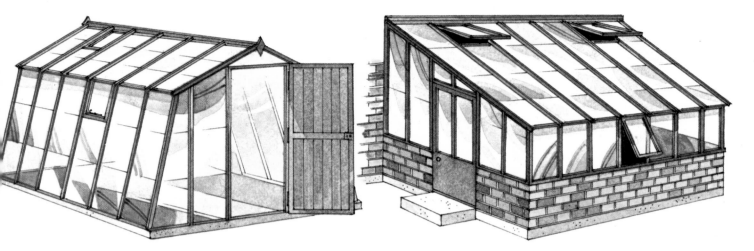

two good reasons: firstly, a very small greenhouse – such as the popular 6 × 8ft (1.8 × 2.4m) – is very quickly filled with plants so that in no time at all you find you do not have enough space. Secondly, a small greenhouse heats up very rapidly in warm weather and it is difficult to keep the temperature down to an acceptable level for plants. It is far easier to control the atmosphere and temperature in a larger house. So if space permits, think in terms of a greenhouse larger than 6 × 8ft (1.8 × 2.4m), and, if possible, buy one that can be extended at a later date.

The basic framework
Timber is the traditional framework material and these days western red cedar is very popular. Softwood framework, in pine or spruce, is also available and somewhat cheaper.

Advantages of timber framework are that the house will be slightly warmer than an aluminum-framed model and condensation will be less of a problem. Also, it is easier to install equipment and, indeed, a timber-framed house is much easier to erect than an aluminum one, as it is supplied in (generally) six sections, which are simply bolted together. Glazing is usually good, with no problems from drafts or leaks. There are one or two disadvantages – timber is not as strong as aluminum and therefore the framework members are thicker, which does slightly cut down on light transmission. Timber has to be treated regularly with preservative or paint to prevent splitting and decay.

Aluminum alloy is used a great deal today for the framework. There are several advantages – it needs no maintenance and the framework members are thinner than those of timber so light transmission is very good. There are some disadvantages. Erection can be very slow and sometimes rather complicated, as there are a great many parts to fit together. There could be more of a problem with condensation building up inside in cool weather. Equipment is not so easy to install, although there are special fixings for such things as insulation material, training wires, etc. Some aluminum houses have an attractive anodized or acrylic finish, but these are more expensive.

Glazing
There is no doubt that glass is the best material for cladding a greenhouse – it ensures excellent light penetration, is easy to clean, does not discolor and will last a lifetime if treated with respect.

Some greenhouses, though, are clad with flexible plastic film or PVC and these are much cheaper than those glazed with horticultural glass. However, it should be borne in mind that these materials have a short life and need replacing every two or three years. They discolor and become brittle. Furthermore, flexible plastic greenhouses lose heat very quickly and condensation can be a great problem if the greenhouse is not ventilated adequately. Plastic films with ultraviolet inhibitors should be chosen, as these have the longest life.

Rigid plastics are also being used more and more for cladding greenhouses and these have slightly better heat retention than flexible kinds and have a much longer life. They may be smooth and glass-like or corrugated.

Shapes of greenhouses
Today, there are many shapes to choose from. The even-span house is the traditional shape with a pitched roof, each side being of equal shape and size. You can choose from models with straight sides or with slightly sloping sides for even better light penetration; and from solid sides to bench height or glass-to-ground, or a combination of the two. Even-span houses with attractively curved eaves have been introduced in recent years.

Above left *Dutch-light style greenhouses are available in timber or aluminum. This design has good light transmission and is a useful general-purpose greenhouse, particularly recommended for vegetable cultivation.*

Above right *Lean-to versions of the traditional even-span houses are becoming increasingly popular and are available with solid sides to bench height or glazed virtually to the ground. Erected against a wall of the dwelling house, they retain heat much better than free-standing greenhouses.*

Circular or lantern-shaped greenhouses, in timber or aluminum, make an attractive garden feature and are used mainly for displaying decorative plants, although crops like tomatoes can be grown in them. Most models are on the small side and if not equipped with plenty of ventilators will become very hot during warm weather. Circular greenhouses are available with glass virtually to the ground or, as shown here, with solid sides to bench height, and they may be six, nine or twelve sided.

The mansard, or curvilinear, greenhouse has the roof panels arranged at various angles to give a somewhat tunnel shape and excellent light transmission. It is an excellent type for displaying plants and for propagation and is available only with aluminum framework and glass-to-ground or solid walls to bench height. A mansard greenhouse is generally wide in relation to its length.

Traditionally, a Dutch light greenhouse is constructed of Dutch frame lights (or covers) bolted together to form an even-span structure with sloping sides. A Dutch light consists of a timber frame, $5 \times 2\frac{1}{2}$ ft (1.5×0.75m) holding a single pane of glass. Such a house has good light transmission and is a useful general-purpose greenhouse, particularly recommended for vegetables. Today, you can build Dutch-light style greenhouses yourself.

Circular greenhouses are available with six, nine or twelve sides – they are really "lantern shaped" and make a nice feature in a garden, useful for displaying plants. Timber or aluminum versions are available, with glass-to-ground or with solid sides to bench height.

The dome-shaped or geodesic greenhouse creates a magnificent garden feature. It has excellent light transmission and plenty of space for displaying plants. It has an aluminum framework and glass almost to ground level.

The uneven-span greenhouse has one high wall, slightly sloping, which should face south. The roof slopes back from this wall. There are timber or aluminum versions and some models are clad with plastic. It is useful for vegetable crops, chrysanthemums, carnations and other plants which like high light intensity and which need plenty of headroom.

There are all kinds of mini-greenhouses available for very tiny gardens, balconies and roof gardens. You cannot get inside them, but access is easy by means of large, sliding or hinged, generally double doors. There are aluminum and timber versions and they are usually glazed to ground level. Mini-greenhouses can heat up rapidly, so ventilate well in warm weather.

Lean-to versions of traditional even-span and mansard houses are available, for erecting against a wall. There are also mini-lean-to houses, ideal for balconies.

Conservatories are available in timber or aluminum and can be supplied in kit form or specially built by several specialist companies. Generally, they have solid brick or timber sides to bench height. It is possible these days to have virtually any size or shape and style to suit the style of your house, as well as your budget.

Polyethylene tunnel greenhouses may be erected on a vegetable plot and used for growing vegetables. They consist of galvanized, tubular-steel hoops which are inserted in the ground and these are covered with flexible sheeting. This is stretched tightly and the edges buried about 18in (45cm) deep in the soil. They are cheap compared with normal greenhouses, but they quickly lose heat and it is much less economical to use artificial heat in them. There is a door at each end, and special tunnel ventilators are also available.

Finally, you can buy a greenhouse and shed combined. It is an even-span structure, divided down the middle, and for many people solves the problem of finding space for two separate buildings.

Siting a greenhouse

Ideally, a free-standing greenhouse should have the ridge running from east to west, but this is not essential, provided it is erected in an open, sunny part of the garden. A house which is shaded for much of the day will severely limit the range of plants that can be grown. A lean-to or conservatory is best sited on a south- or west-facing wall.

The greenhouse should be well sheltered from wind – cold winds will quickly lower the temperature inside the house and so it will be more expensive to heat. If necessary, erect a windbreak on the windward side – but some distance from the house – using windbreak netting, or plant a screen of conifers or hedging shrubs. If your garden is sloping do not erect a greenhouse at the bottom of the slope, for cold air drains down and forms a frost pocket. In this extra-cold spot, heating bills will be higher. Position the greenhouse halfway up a slope if possible.

If plants are to be grown in soil borders in the greenhouse, then choose a piece of ground that is well drained and reasonably fertile, to avoid problems later.

You may wish to run water, electricity or gas to the greenhouse, in which case it is sensible to site it as close as possible to the house, for the cost of running such services is generally very high and increases dramatically as distance increases.

Planning permission from local authorities is not generally needed for a free-standing greenhouse, unless is it to be an exceptionally large structure, in which case it would be advisable to discuss the matter with the planning department first. It is advisable to get planning permission for a lean-to or conservatory and may even be essential if there is to be access from the house. You may find it sensible to seek the advice of an architect or local builder.

CHAPTER 2

BUILDING A GREENHOUSE

Building a greenhouse can appear daunting at first, but if you follow the manufacturer's instructions carefully, and proceed in the order recommended, you shouldn't go wrong. Building your own will save you money, and you know that the job's well done.

Before ordering, let alone erecting, a lean-to greenhouse or conservatory, planning permission may be needed. Generally there are no problems, but the structure must be erected on a substantial base. Timber-framed structures are easier and quicker to put up than those with aluminum frame sections.

Free-standing greenhouse

Having decided on a greenhouse, and before it is delivered, the chosen site must be leveled. Use wooden pegs, a straight-edge board and spirit level. The first peg is inserted into the ground until the top is at the desired level. Then you work from this peg in all directions over the site, inserting pegs about 3ft (1m) apart, and using the board and spirit level to ensure all the tops are at the same level as the original peg.

The next step is to add or take away soil as necessary so that the soil level over the entire site corresponds with the tops of all the pegs.

The greenhouse base

Manufacturers these days may supply pre-fabricated bases for their greenhouses; these can be precast concrete, steel and extra-strong plastic. There is generally a post or stake of some kind bolted to each corner, and these have to be concreted into the ground. The base is simply laid on the prepared level site, ensuring the soil is really firm. The manufacturer's instructions will advise how the base should be laid. It is essential that the corners of the base are at right angles or the framework of the house will not fit. This can be assured by using a large set square. Generally, the greenhouse framework is bolted to this base and again instructions will tell you how.

To make your own base, first mark out the area of the greenhouse, using four wooden pegs and string. Then make a trench all around the outline, the depth and width of a spade. This is half filled with brick rubble and firmed.

Bricks are then placed at each corner, one on each side, and these must all be level, ensured by using a spirit level and straight-edge board. The tops of the bricks represent the final level of the concrete.

Fill up the trench to the level of the bricks with concrete – five parts sand to one part cement. When this has set, a single row of bricks can be laid on which to stand the greenhouse, bedding them on mortar – four parts builders' sand to one part cement. They must be perfectly level, so use a spirit level while laying. Metal coach bolts should be inserted into the mortar between the bricks, about 3ft (1m) apart, in order to hold down the greenhouse framework. A damp-proof course can be provided by laying a strip of bituminized roofing felt over the bricks. If you are buying a greenhouse which requires brick walls to bench height, then continue building up with bricks to the specified height.

Assembling the framework

You can either put up the house yourself or make use of one of the erection services recommended by the manufacturer. Timber greenhouses are often easier to erect than

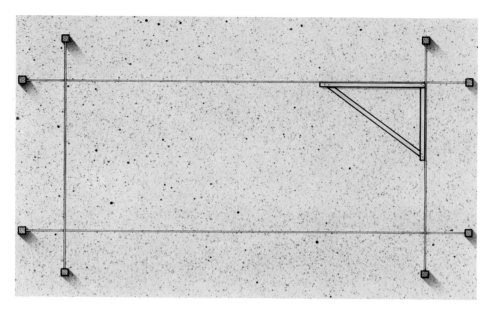

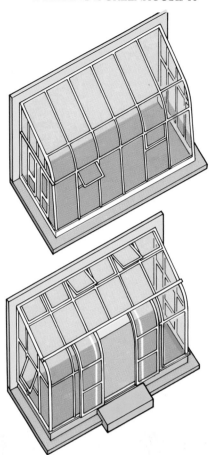

aluminum ones, as they are supplied in sections which are simply bolted together. Some houses are even pre-glazed. Aluminum houses are supplied in many parts and you will have packages of glazing bars, vents, doors, etc. The manufacturer's instructions must be carefully studied before unpacking and making a start. Ideally, a greenhouse should be erected by two people – it makes the job easier.

The floor

Most gardeners simply have a path down the center of the house with soil borders on either side, over which benches could be erected, of course. A path is easily made with a row of concrete paving slabs, laid on 6in (15cm) of well-rammed rubble topped with builders' sand. Bed each slab on a mix of sand and cement. If you do not wish to grow plants in the soil beds, the soil can be covered with a layer of pea gravel or horticultural aggregate. First cover the soil with a sheet of thick polyethylene to prevent weeds from growing through.

Lean-to greenhouse

Before placing an order for a lean-to greenhouse or conservatory, contact your local building inspector to discuss the models you have short-listed. Most manufacturers supply plans for this purpose. Planning regulations for lean-to greenhouses or conservatories can be complicated, but, on the other hand, most people experience few problems and the building inspector will advise you. There are certain general regulations – for instance, the concrete floor slab must be sufficiently deep around its perimeter; there must be enough opening windows; and it cannot be too near a public highway. If you intend erecting the lean-to green-

house or conservatory yourself, you will still be subject to an increase in the local tax assessment on your property in most communities.

Possible problems

When you have chosen a lean-to greenhouse or conservatory, but before ordering, mark out the area it will occupy. Mark with chalk the estimated level of the concrete slab and draw a line indicating where the structure would attach to the house – the ridge height and sides.

Now consider if there are any problems – do any windows or doors breach the line? If so, you may need a higher structure, or to raise the level of the slab. The level of the concrete slab must not be higher than the damp-proof course of the house. The damp-proof course of the slab can be at the same level or lower than the damp course of the house.

To save a lot of problems later, the position of the structure may have to be shifted slightly to avoid, say, rainwater pipes, inspection covers, drain covers, traps or gullies. Try to find out where underground pipes or drains are likely to run. They can be protected from the weight of the slab by encasing them in concrete.

When you have finally decided on model and site, you will need to contact your building inspector concerning planning permission and building approval. Submit the manufacturer's drawings and specifications, and a plan of your house and garden, with the proposed conservatory marked in. Do wait for approval before any work is undertaken.

Preparing the foundations

The lean-to greenhouse or conservatory is built on a concrete slab or base, which

Top left *The lean-to greenhouse or conservatory is built on a concrete slab or base, which should first be marked out with pegs and string, using the dimensions supplied by the manufacturer.*

Top *Conservatories or lean-tos at the lower end of the market are supplied with a minimum of useful accessories, and often do not have enough ventilators.*

Above *Better models, though, include plenty of ventilators, a choice of door positions, guttering and various accessories.*

1. *The finished floor height should be marked on the house wall; then a second mark, 2in (5cm) below this, should be made to indicate the height of the main concrete slab.*

2. *The soil is then excavated to accommodate the concrete, but try to avoid or re-route underground pipes rather than building on top of them. However, this is not always possible.*

3. *Lay 4in (10cm) of gravel in the excavation, but leave the foundation trench (around the edge) empty. Then add a layer of sand and rake it flat.*

4. *Before laying the concrete, a strip of plastic sheeting spread against the house wall will prevent unsightly splashes and act as an extra prevention against damp.*

should first be marked out with pegs and string, using the dimensions supplied by the manufacturer. Mark the finished floor height in chalk on the house wall, then make a second mark 2in (5cm) below this for the height of the main slab.

Excavate the soil to a depth of 12in (30cm) below the level of the finished slab. A deeper trench is then dug around the inside edge of the excavation, about 6in (15cm) deeper, as the slab edges must be thicker.

Before laying the gravel, exposed drainpipes will need encasing with concrete. Traps will need similar support. A bolt-down double seal cover plate will have to be added to any trap or inspection chamber. It must lie flush with the final floor finish.

The edges of the excavation should be lined with formwork – boarding fixed to stakes – to hold the concrete in place as it sets. Boarding should be level with the main slab height and 6in (15cm) or more below ground level. The stakes should be inserted on the outside of the perimeter line and the boards nailed to them.

Lay 4in (10cm) of gravel in the excavation – broken bricks, etc – tamp it down level and make sure it is reasonably firm. Add a layer of sand and rake it flat. If the building inspector asks for it, now is the time to add reinforcing mesh – support it, with bits of brick, 2in (5cm) above the level of the sand.

You are now ready to lay the concrete but carry out these final checks: will the slab be large enough for the conservatory frame to overlap its edges slightly? Is there sufficient depth for 8in (20cm) of concrete below finished slab level? Is the foundation trench 12in (30cm) deep and wide?

Laying the concrete slab

You will need much more concrete than can conveniently be mixed by hand, so you will have to decide if you want to buy in ready-mixed concrete or hire a cement mixer for the job.

Whichever method you choose, you will have to work out the volume of material needed for the main slab, using the formula one part portland cement to two parts sharp concreting sand and three parts aggregate. To help you get a sense of proportion, a bag of cement weighs roughly 1cwt (50kg). Adding to this the two parts of sand, about 2cwt (100kg) and three parts of aggregate, about 3cwt (150kg) will give you 6 cu ft (0.17 cu m) of concrete.

Calculating how much concrete you need requires a rough plan of the slab and the trench foundations combined. The calculation is made by multiplying the slab width by the length by the depth. Here is a sample calculation: slab – 6½ft wide × 8½ft long × ½ft deep = 27½ = slab volume 27½cu ft. To this is added the volume of the trench,

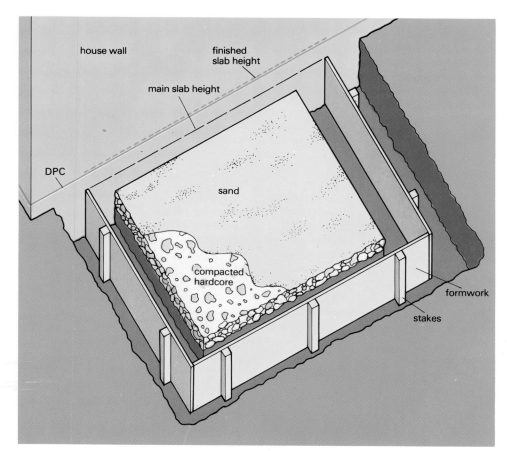

Left *This is the ideal excavation for the concrete slab: timber formwork is level with the main slab height. Extra formwork for the screed layer is added on top later.*

Below *Calculating how much concrete you need requires a rough plan of the the slab and the trench foundations combined. See sample calculation given on these pages.*

calculated in the same way as previously. Here is a sample calculation. Trench – (6½ft + 6½ft + 8½ft) = 21½ft × 1ft × 1ft = 21½ft = trench 21½cu ft. Total = 27½ + 21½ = 49cu ft. Divide the total volume by the known yield of one bag of cement, two of sand and three of aggregate to work out the amount of each item. In this particular instance, four bags of cement, eight bags of sand and twelve bags of aggregate are the minimum needed.

The tools you will need are a wooden float, and for a really smooth finish a steel float, a shovel and a spirit level. You will also need a screeding board for compacting and leveling the concrete, which is easily made from a long sturdy 3 × 3in (7.5 × 7.5cm) timber with 2 × 1in (5 × 2.5cm) battens nailed to the ends for handles. The board must be long enough to stretch from one side of the slab to the other.

Before laying the concrete, a strip of plastic sheeting spread against the house wall will prevent unsightly splashes and act as an extra prevention against damp. Spread this the length of the slab and from the bottom of the excavation to about 24in (60cm) above its finished height, then tack it in place. Leave it while you cast the slab.

To mix your own concrete, pour a liberal amount of water into the bowl of the concrete mixer then add the aggregate and sand and give them time to mix. Finally add

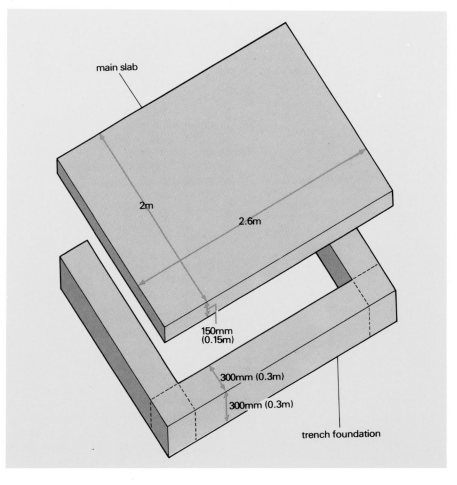

The use of a screeding board will work the concrete flat and consolidate it. A combination of scraping and chopping motions produces this result. With large areas of concrete it is best for two people to handle the screeding board. The surface will have a slight rippled effect — leave it to settle for an hour, then smooth it flat with a wooden float.

the cement and gradually more water until you have a plastic consistency. Make sure the mix is not runny. If you have put in too much water, add more of the dry ingredients in the same proportions.

A useful tip is to make an open-bottomed box about 24in (60cm) square and 10in (25cm) deep so that you can measure each ingredient by volume. Each load counts as one measure.

Spread the concrete into the excavation, starting from the house side and working to the position nearest the mixing place. A garden rake or shovel can be used to spread the concrete. Tamp it down well, especially into the foundation trenches. If reinforcing mesh has been laid, take hold of it at regular intervals and give it a good shaking up and down to consolidate the concrete around it.

Continue laying, spreading and compacting the concrete until it is about ½in (12mm) above the top of the formwork. Then, with the aid of a helper, work your screeding board over the surface of the concrete, using the formwork as a guide to level. With a combination of scraping and chopping motions, work the concrete flat and consolidate it by scraping away from the house wall. Add more concrete as the level goes down. Finish off with a series of light sweeps with the screeding board.

The surface will have a slight rippled effect – leave it to settle for an hour then smooth it flat with a wooden float.

Damp proofing and screed

Once the concrete slab has set, the next stage is to provide a continuous damp-proof membrane. This is tucked into the damp-proof course in the house wall. Finally a 2in (5cm) screen of finer concrete is laid to bring the slab to its final height and to give you a really smooth and pleasing finish.

The damp-proof membrane is a sheet of heavy-duty polyethylene that should cover the whole of the slab and be joined to the existing damp-proof course – that is, if you have one. The edges of the sheet are trimmed off after the final screed has been laid and has hardened. It is essential that the damp-proof membrane is a single sheet, and of course it must have no holes in it.

First release the strip of polyethylene you tacked to the wall and fold it back onto the slab. Using a bolster or an old screwdriver, remove the damp-proof course in the wall to a depth of about 1½in (4cm). If there is no damp-proof course (it looks like a layer of black tar), then rake out the course of mortar instead.

Spread out the new polyethylene. It must overlap the edges of the slab. The edge nearest the house wall should be slipped into the groove you have raked out. It should be sealed in place with mastic – work it well into the mortar course.

Finally, you can lay the screed. First, nail a frame of 2 × 1in (5 × 2.5cm) timber to the top of the formwork, sandwiching the edges of the damp-proof membrane. The inner surface of the new frame should be in line with the edge of the concrete slab. It should be secured with strips of timber nailed to the outside.

It is easier when screeding to divide the slab area into smaller, more manageable areas, using 2 × 1in (5 × 2.5cm) wooden battens, nailed to the formwork. A screeding mix should be made up of one part cement to three parts sharp sand. Start laying it at the wall, completing one area at a time. The screeding board should be used to scrape and tamp it down. To achieve a really smooth surface, finish off with the steel float.

When the first area is dry, remove the battens and lay the second area. Use the edge of the first area as formwork and as an edge for the screeding board. Allow the screed to dry before the formwork is removed. Trim the exposed edges of the damp-proof membrane. Backfill around the edge of the slab.

Dealing with traps and gullies

If you cannot easily reposition drainage traps and gullies or inspection chambers you will have to incorporate them into the concrete slab. It means building an airtight brick box around the trap or gully and fitting a double-seal cast iron cover – obtainable from building suppliers. The cover lies flush with the floor. Choose a cover that is bigger than the existing cover. Build up the brick box to the intended level of the top of the main slab. Cast the main slab around the box and lay the damp-proof membrane over the edges of the brick box. Place the frame of the double seal cover over the top of the box and pack up the four

Below left *Before laying the screed, cover the concrete with a damp-proof membrane and add more timber to the top of the existing formwork.*

Below right *If it is not possible to relocate traps or gullies they will have to be built into the slab. They must be airtight but accessible so a double-seal cover will be necessary. The brick "box" is built before the slab is cast.*

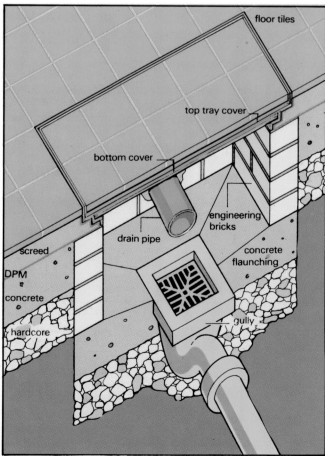

1. *The conservatory or lean-to is assembled in a specific sequence. Generally the main sections – walls, roof, door, etc – are assembled on a flat piece of ground.*

2. *The main framework is then bolted together: it is often easiest to up-end the frame to add roof sections, ridge, etc.*

3. *In many aluminum structures, rubber sealing strips are used and generally these are added before the framework is assembled.*

4. *If there is a gap of more than 1in (2.5cm) between framework and wall in places, a shaped wooden batten will be needed to provide a square edge. Bitumen tape forms a waterproof seal.*

5. *The glazing starts with the roof and then proceeds to the front and ends.*

6. *Door locks and window catches generally bolt on through pre-drilled holes.*

corners with cement until the frame is level. Lay the screed in the normal way. The screed must be pressed under the raised edges of the frame.

Assembling the frame
When the lean-to greenhouse or conservatory is delivered, unpack and check the contents against the list supplied, but keep all the parts in their original cartons. Then carefully read the assembly instructions, preferably several times, until you fully understand them.

The conservatory will be assembled in a specific sequence; this will vary according to make, but the instructions will, of course, advise on this. Generally the main sections – walls, roof, doors, etc – are assembled on a flat piece of ground and the main framework is then bolted together on the concrete base.

To start with, all nuts and bolts and other fixings are screwed to finger tightness. Only when the main framework is fully assembled on its base, and you are sure that it is perfectly squared up and everything fits as it should do, should you fully tighten all nuts and bolts, etc.

It is a good idea to have some trestles and planks nearby. Using them, you can work on higher parts of the greenhouse frame with relative ease, and without the distraction of worrying about losing or dropping the various components.

Position the main framework on a special prefabricated base if one has been supplied, according to instructions. Check that all is square, and that the framework butts up to the wall all round, then carry out final tightening.

Small irregularities between frame and wall will be rectified by waterproof seals. However, if there is a gap of more than 1in (2.5cm) in places, a shaped wooden batten will be needed to provide a square edge.

The base of the framework should be screwed down first: place a layer of non-setting mastic beneath it. A layer of bitumen tape is placed between the frame and the wall to form a weatherproof seal. The framework is then screwed to the wall, using masonary plugs and, ideally, rust-resistant screws.

Glazing the frame
Again, manufacturer's instructions should be followed regarding sequence and bedding the glass in the glazing bars. Usually, special sealing strips are used. Sub-frames, such as doors and ventilators, are generally glazed first, and then fitted after the main glazing has been completed. The main glazing starts with the roof and then proceeds to the front and ends.

After glazing, the structure can be tested for leaks by spraying it, including the wall,

3

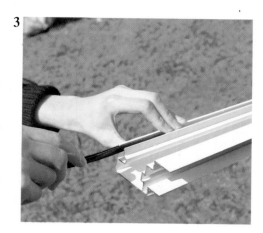

6

with a hose and any leaks can be sealed, when dry, with a clear silicone sealant, although if the conservatory is well made, and you have assembled and glazed it correctly, there really should be no leaks.

Installing a dry well

Most conservatories and greenhouses are supplied with gutters and downpipes and if these cannot discharge into an existing drain you will have to build a dry well. Specifications and siting can be obtained from your building inspector. However, it basically consists of a pit at least 13ft (4m) from the nearest buildings, and filled with gravel or rubble.

The rainwater from the gutters drains along an underground pipe into the dry well, where it gradually seeps into the subsoil.

The underground pipe at the conservatory end can be connected to a new trapped gully where the downpipe can discharge above the grating.

Dig a trench for the underground pipe, about 10in (25cm) wide, and progressively deep enough to give the recommended fall between the trap and dry well. The pit can be filled with rubble or gravel. Use lengths of UPVC underground pipe between the gully and pit. The top of the dry well can be covered with concrete paving slabs to prevent soil washing down into it.

Finishing off

The most exciting part for most people is finishing off the interior of the greenhouse or conservatory. Consider firstly the floor. For a conservatory, the covering can be as simple as rush matting, which can look most attractive. Or you could be more ambitious and lay floor tiles, either vinyl or ceramic kinds. They will be easy to lay on the smooth level finish of the screed.

However, for a more functional greenhouse floor, you may wish to leave the screed as it is – after all, it makes a perfectly good floor. Remember, you must seal it first to prevent a dusty or powdery surface. It is possible to buy clear cement sealants for this purpose. Alternatively, paint it with flooring paint – there is a reasonably wide choice of colors available.

The rear wall can be painted a light color to reflect the light, and to give the structure the appearance of belonging to the house rather than being merely tacked on. White or cream is a good, reflective color for the wall.

Lighting will be needed and the best type consists of fluorescent tubes – but unless you are a competent electrician, leave this job to a qualified professional.

Equipment, such as extra ventilators, heating and automatic watering systems will need to be considered and these are discussed in Chapter Three.

Climbing plants can be grown on the back wall, trained to trellis panels of timber or plastic-coated steel, or even to horizontal wires placed 12in (30cm) apart and fixed to the wall by means of masonary vine eyes. Leave a gap of about 1½in (4cm) between trellis or wires and the wall to ensure good air circulation. Pot plants can be grown on benches (generally supplied as an optional extra by the manufacturer of the greenhouse or conservatory) at the front and side, and larger, more permanent plants – shrubs, palms, citrus fruits, camellias, bird of paradise flowers – could be grown in large ornamental tubs and other containers. Hanging baskets could probably be secured from the roof framework.

Do not forget to landscape the outside of the building. This is a matter of personal choice: for instance, you may wish to have grass right up to the building, with a path leading from the door to the main garden path. Or you may like to have a patio alongside it, on which you could stand pots and urns of colorful spring and summer bedding plants. There is no reason why you should not have a narrow border around the building, again planted with spring and summer bedding, with winter-flowering bulbs for additional color.

CHAPTER 3
HEATING, WATERING & VENTILATION

The environment inside a greenhouse is entirely artificial, and it is up to you to provide the plants with the heat, water and fresh air that they need to thrive. Getting the balance right to start with is not difficult, and gets easier with practice.

Below A greenhouse can today be completely automated so that it may be left unattended for varying periods. Ventilation, shading, watering and heating can all be automatic. However, if you are at home all day it really is better to keep a close eye on the greenhouse and look after plants according to weather conditions.

Opposite Heating pipes should ideally run underneath benches so that plants benefit from the rising warm air. Deep benches as shown here allow plants to be plunged in a moisture-retentive medium, such as sand or peat, to prevent rapid drying out.

Controlling the environment

The greenhouse gardener must create and control the environment under glass to suit the plants being grown. This means providing the right temperature, adequate ventilation, shading from strong sunshine and water in the right amounts.

Today, much of this can be automated, so that the gardener does not have to keep a constant eye on the greenhouse, and indeed the house can be left for several days if it is well equipped.

Artificial heating increases the range of plants that can be grown and allows you to make an early start with plant raising, such as food crops and summer bedding plants. Unless you are growing tropical plants, it is not necessary to heat the house to a high temperature – most gardeners provide heat from early autumn to late spring.

Due to the high cost of heating, most gardeners these days maintain cool conditions in their greenhouses – a minimum temperature of 40°F (4.5°C). In this you can grow flowering pot plants all the year round, raise bedding and food plants, over-winter tender plants and have food crops available throughout the year. A minimum temperature of 50°F (10°C) enables a wider range of plants to be grown, including some of the sub-tropical kinds. A warm greenhouse has a minimum temperature of 60°F (15.5°C) and here tropical plants can be grown throughout the year.

A stuffy atmosphere must be avoided at all times, and therefore a greenhouse must be ventilated. You should aim for a buoyant atmosphere, which means that the right temperature is being maintained, yet there is a regular air change in the house, so that the air is always fresh. A greenhouse must, therefore, be well equipped with ventilators. Many houses do not have sufficient vents, but manufacturers generally offer ventilators as optional extras, and it is always a good idea to order a few extra when placing an order for the greenhouse.

In temperate climates, plants need to be shaded from strong sunshine between mid-spring and early autumn. Shading prevents leaves from being scorched, seedlings from being "burnt up," helps to prevent the compost and soil drying out rapidly, and helps to keep the temperature down during very warm weather. It is possible to have too high a temperature for greenhouse plants, usually from 95°F (35°C) upward.

Heating equipment

There are four main types of heating available – kerosene, gas, electricity and solid fuel. Among the most economical are kerosene and solid fuel, with gas and electricity being the most expensive.

Kerosene heaters

There is a wide range available – from very small to large heaters capable of keeping a 20 × 10ft (6 × 3m) greenhouse frost free. The best type of kerosene heater is one with a blue-flame burner as opposed to models with a yellow-flame burner. The former are more efficient and there is less risk of fumes being produced.

The simplest kerosene heaters are metal boxes which release their heat from holes in the top. More advanced types have pipes or ducts which distribute heat more efficiently. These are suitable for heating large houses, or for maintaining high temperatures in small structures. Kerosene heaters can be partly automated, by feeding fuel from a large drum by gravity to the heater's supply tank by means of plastic tubing. The drum can, of course, be positioned outside the greenhouse.

The advantages of kerosene heaters are that they are comparatively cheap to buy and run, they are portable and provide carbon-dioxide – beneficial to plants. There are some disadvantages. Regular attention is needed, as they must be kept clean and the wick trimmed regularly to prevent harmful fumes from being produced. The burning fuel produces water vapor which can lead to condensation, and some ventilation must be provided at all times.

Gas heaters

These are becoming quite popular now and basically they consist of a portable warm-air cabinet which emits heat from the top. Gas heaters are thermostatically controlled so they can safely be left unattended.

There are two types – natural gas and bottled gas. The former is relatively cheaper to run than bottled-gas types, but running a gas supply to a greenhouse can be costly. It is best installed and connected by a professional gas fitter. The bottled-gas heaters run off propane or butane gas, supplied in cylinders. Buy large cylinders as they work out more economical in the long run.

Gas gives off beneficial carbon-dioxide, and the heaters need the minimum of attention and maintenance. The burning fuel gives off water vapor as with kerosene, so watch out for condensation and ventilate the greenhouse accordingly.

Electric heaters

Electricity is the most efficient fuel – there is absolutely no wastage and, as heaters are thermostatically controlled, an electric heating system can be left unattended for long periods. Other advantages are that most heaters are very reliable, portable, and all give off dry heat so there are no condensation problems in winter. The disadvantages are that electricity is an expensive fuel and the cost of running a supply to the greenhouse can be high. Also, you will need an emergency heater (kerosene, for example), to use in the event of a power cut. It is advisable to have a professional electrician install the power supply, control panel and other such parts.

There are various types to choose from, the most popular being the fan heaters which blow out warm air and keep the greenhouse air circulating well.

Tubular heaters consist of hollow tubes, each containing a heating element, and these are mounted in "banks" on a wall of the greenhouse, the number depending on the amount of heat needed. They can be installed under the benches if desired.

Electric convection heaters basically consist of a cabinet; cold air is drawn in from the bottom, is heated in the cabinet,

Below left *Whether you have a large or small greenhouse it can be heated with a kerosene heater. Unfortunately, this method is not as cheap as it used to be and indeed kerosene is quite expensive, but more economical than, say, electricity.*

Below right *There are various types of electric heaters to choose from, including tubular heaters, which are generally mounted beneath the benches so that warm air rises all around the plants.*

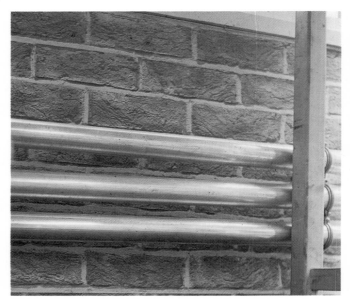

and emerges, warmed, at the top. An advantage is that the greenhouse air is kept moving. Convection heaters are particularly suited to the larger greenhouse.

Electric soil-warming cables are bedded in the soil, or in sand on the greenhouse benches, and provide localized heat – that is, at soil or root level. They do very little to heat the atmosphere, but "bottom heat" is very useful for early planting (tomatoes, for example), and for propagation, like seed raising and rooting cuttings. Warming cables are cheaper to run than other electrical systems, but you will need another heater to warm the air in the greenhouse. Make sure you buy a soil-warming system with thermostatic control – not all have this facility.

Solid fuel systems

This is the traditional way of heating greenhouses, and consists of a boiler with hot-water pipes running around the walls of the greenhouse. The boiler is placed outside, but under cover. This is an ideal system if you want to maintain high temperatures in your greenhouse with economical running costs. Modern boilers need minimum attention, but of course there will be daily stoking and ash clearing. Dry heat is given off from the pipes so no condensation problems occur. A solid-fuel system is suitable for small or large greenhouses, and manufacturers will advise on the size you need and the types of fuel which can be used. Modern boilers often burn cheap-grade fuel.

Size of heater

Manufacturers will advise on the size of heater needed for your greenhouse, if you tell them the minimum temperature you wish to maintain. To conserve heat, and therefore reduce fuel bills, do insulate the inside of your greenhouse: one very popular and effective material is bubble plastic and most greenhouse manufacturers can supply special fittings to secure this to the greenhouse framework.

Watering equipment

While some gardeners prefer hand watering, with a watering can, more and more people are turning to automatic watering systems so that they can leave their greenhouse unattended for a few days. This is fine during spring and summer, but plants will need less water in autumn and winter and therefore the automatic system is best shut down during these periods and plants hand watered as they need it.

Ideally, you will need a supply of piped water to the greenhouse. There are two basic methods of automatic watering and one of these is the trickle irrigation system,

suitable for watering soil beds and/or plants in pots. The water is distributed, via a main pipe, to small-bore flexible plastic tubes, each with a controllable nozzle to regulate the amount of water given. This system can be fully automatic, running from a header tank fitted with a ballcock valve, and connected to the piped water supply. A semi-automatic system runs from a header tank or some other kind of reservoir, which has to be filled manually. But it can be left for several days unattended. Yet other systems are connected to a tap by means of a rubber hose, and you just turn on the tap when you want plants watered. None of these is selective, and all plants are watered whether or not they need it, but this is no problem during warm weather.

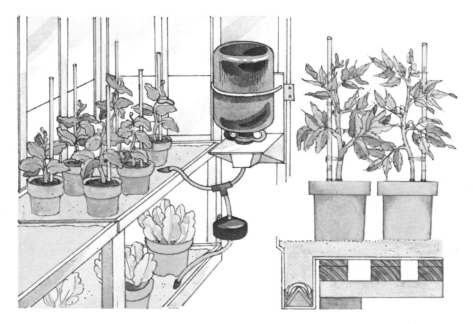

Top *This is a fully automatic trickle watering system which runs from the piped water supply, via a header tank fitted with a ballcock valve. Like all automatic or semi-automatic systems it is best used only during spring and summer when plants need plenty of water.*

Above *The capillary watering system for pot plants is very popular and can be fully automatic (connected to the piped water supply via a header tank), or semi-automatic as shown here, whereby water is supplied from a reservoir bottle which needs to be filled by hand.*

Overhead sprinklers and misting systems are also available, and are either connected to a tap or to a header tank connected to the piped supply. They are useful for damping down greenhouses, especially where high humidity is needed, as when growing cucumbers out of season.

The second type of automatic watering system is known as capillary watering, whereby potted plants are placed on some kind of water-retentive material, and they take up water when they need it. This material may be special capillary matting (something like carpet underlay) or sand. The latter will need extra-strong benches, but matting is very light in weight. Plants should be grown in clay pots and there must be perfect contact between the bottom of the pot and the matting or sand. The matting or sand can be kept moist in several ways – via a pipe, connected to a header tank or some other kind of reservoir, or from a tank/ballcock valve connected direct to the piped water supply. You can either make up your own capillary watering system or buy a complete kit ready to assemble. In the simplest capillary system, water is supplied from a gutter running along the length of the benches, with one edge of the capillary matting dangling in it to draw up the water as needed.

Ventilating equipment

All greenhouses and conservatories are fitted with ventilators, but generally there are not enough. It's best to order a few extra when buying the greenhouse.

Every greenhouse or conservatory needs roof or ridge ventilators and side ventilators. A minimum number of each is one every 6½ ft (2m) length of the structure. If you have a very long greenhouse, then continuous vents, which run the length of the greenhouse, are recommended. The area of roof ventilators must be equal to at least one-sixth of the floor area of the house. The roof vents are generally hinged at the ridge of the greenhouse, and side vents are also generally hinged, but are positioned quite near to the ground. This arrangement allows good air circulation in the building – air is drawn in at the bottom, rises through the house and escapes from the roof vents.

An alternative to the normal hinged side ventilator is the louver vent, with adjustable glass panels so that you can regulate the air intake. They can be a bit drafty. Louver vents replace panes of glass, so it is possible to install as many as you need. Most greenhouse manufacturers are able to supply louver vents for their particular houses.

Automatic ventilation

Hinged ridge and side ventilators can either be opened and closed by hand or fitted with an automatic ventilator arm which will open and close them according to the temperature. If vents are fitted with these, you can completely forget about ventilation, at least in warm weather. In the autumn and winter it may be best to disconnect them and

Below left *An alternative to hinged side ventilators are the louver vents supplied by most greenhouse manufacturers. The glass panels are adjustable so that you can regulate the air intake. They can be automatically controlled by fitting automatic ventilator arms.*

Below right *Electric fans can be used in conjunction with roof and side ventilators and they have the advantage that they keep the air moving and therefore fresh. There are two types: extractor fans which expel warm air and draw in cool air, and circulating types, as shown here, which simply keep the air moving.*

operate vents by hand, for you may need to provide some ventilation in cool or cold weather, when the automatic openers would not operate. More recently, automatic ventilator openers have become available for louver vents.

Automatic ventilator openers are reasonably priced and so it is perfectly feasible to fit them to all ventilators. Some do not need a power source as they are operated by natural heat. Most can be set to open at specific temperatures.

Electric fans can also be used for ventilation. There are simple circulating fans, which keep the greenhouse air moving, and these are mounted in the roof, ideally at the opposite end to the door. Extractor fans are placed in a similar position, and they expel warm air and draw in cool air from outside, particularly useful in hot summer weather. Both circulating fans and extractor fans should be used in conjunction with roof and side ventilators and either kind equally can be recommended for both small and large types of greenhouses.

Shading materials

The simplest way of providing shade is to paint the outside of the glass with a proprietary liquid shading material, the best color being white. Modern kinds let in more light when rain makes them wet (it is generally dull when it is raining and therefore as much light as possible is needed in the greenhouse). When dry, as in warm, sunny weather, the shading is more dense.

Another way to shade greenhouse plants is to fix external roller blinds, which are pulled up and down as required. Various materials are available: wooden laths, plastic reeds, shading netting and some plastic fabric. It is possible, though expensive, to have fully automatic roller blinds, operated by an electric motor.

Internal roller blinds are also available; choose white polyethylene (not green) or polypropylene netting. There is also a polyester sliding system, whereby the blind is slung from a system of wires and can be pulled backwards and forwards (from one end of the house to the other).

Above left *Every greenhouse or conservatory needs ridge and side ventilators. Air is drawn in through the side vents, rises through the house and escapes via the roof vents. This ensures good air circulation, which is so necessary to keep plants healthy and free from damp-loving diseases.*

Above right *Automatic ventilators may be controlled by temperature and therefore an electricity supply is not needed. They can be fitted to roof, side and louver vents.*

Above *Roller blinds made of wooden laths are the traditional way of shading a greenhouse and there is still nothing to beat them for durability. If you decide you can afford it, they can be automatically controlled by means of electric winding gear.*

CHAPTER 4

MANAGEMENT & MAINTENANCE

The day-to-day care in managing a greenhouse involves similar skills to managing a home. It must be kept clean, with heat, shading and fresh air according to season, the inhabitants must be fed and watered and treated against the occasional illnesses that occur.

Equipment and accessories

Relatively inexpensive compared to the initial cost of a greenhouse, equipment and accessories are worth investing in. Buy the best you can afford, to keep your repair and replacement costs down to a minimum.

Benching

Plants are raised, and pot plants are grown, on some form of benching, which in greenhouse-gardening terms is really important. There are two main reasons for using benches. They allow you to position plants in maximum light (there is often less light at floor level, especially in houses with partially solid sides). Benches also enable you to make maximum use of space, for some plants, particularly shade-loving kinds, can be grown underneath the supports, and dormant or resting plants and bulbs can be stored underneath, too.

Benches are often placed down one side of the house, for pot plants, and on the other side a soil border is made, for growing tall crops like tomatoes, peppers, chrysanthemums and carnations.

Many manufacturers supply benches for their greenhouses: in aluminum if you have an aluminum-framed house, or in timber if it is timber framed. Some benches come as a single tier, but it is possible to also buy several tiers, ideal for displaying ornamental plants.

There is a choice of bench surfaces. With slatted or openwork beneath, surplus water drains rapidly, there is excellent air circulation around plants and heat is able to rise through the openings. It is specially recommended for many pot plants, including pelargoniums and orchids.

Benches can also be supplied with gravel trays, which are filled with horticultural aggregate, shingle or gravel. These can also be filled with sand for capillary watering. If the trays are filled with gravel or aggregate, keep this moist in warm weather to create a humid atmosphere around suitable plants.

If you wish to use capillary matting on the benches, slatted staging must be covered with something solid, to prevent the matting from sagging through the slats – for instance, marine plywood or perhaps spare timber planks.

The main level of benching is generally about 3ft (1m) high and a maximum width is also 3ft (1m). Always leave a gap of 1–2in (2.5–5cm) between benches and the side of the greenhouse to allow warm air to rise behind it and for air circulation. Some kinds of benching can be easily dismantled and removed to make more room for summer crops such as cucumbers, tomatoes, peppers and eggplants.

Shelving

Again, many greenhouse manufacturers supply shelving, which can be put up in the roof area or fixed to the back wall. As shelving is placed in good light, it is useful for holding trays of seedlings or cuttings in the spring.

Propagating case

If you have an electricity supply to your greenhouse it is well worthwhile investing in an electrically heated propagating case for raising seeds and rooting cuttings – and also for starting off tender bulbs, corms and tubers, such as begonias. All of these techniques require high temperatures – in the region of 65–70°F (18–21°C) – and of course it is totally out of the question for most people to provide this temperature range in the rest of the greenhouse. An electric propagator will provide this range of temperatures and the heat will be where it is needed – at the soil level. Many propagators only cost a few cents a week to run, especially if they include a built-in thermostat. There are many sizes, from very small (perhaps holding only one seed tray) to large, which can hold at least half a dozen trays of seeds. Buy the largest your greenhouse can accommodate.

Today, greenhouse benches are often very flexible, allowing you to remove or lift the decking if you want to grow tall crops like tomatoes at soil level. This saves the need to remove all the framework as well.

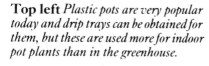

Top left *Plastic pots are very popular today and drip trays can be obtained for them, but these are used more for indoor pot plants than in the greenhouse.*

Top right *Clay pots were once the only type available. They went out of favor when plastic pots came in, but are now becoming popular again, possibly due to the fact that many gardeners find them easier to manage. There is not so much risk of keeping plants too wet in clay pots for the soil dries out more quickly.*

Left *There are all sorts of pieces of propagation equipment available to the greenhouse gardener. The most useful is a propagating case (shown top), ideally electrically heated. An alternative is a glass fish tank (top right). A heated propagating base (bottom right) is among the more economical pieces of equipment. Failing any of these, cuttings or seeds can be covered with glass domes or jars, with sheets of glass, or with clear plastic bags, as shown in the remainder of the photograph.*

Pots

There are many different kinds of pot to choose from, each with particular advantages. **Plastic pots** are the most widely used today and are available in a wide range of sizes. The soils do not dry out so rapidly in these as they do in clay pots, so be careful not to overwater.

Clay pots are coming back into favor after a period of neglect. Soils do dry out more quickly in these, so keep a close eye on water requirements, particularly in warm weather. Many people consider them to be much more attractive than their plastic counterparts. They are, however, more expensive especially the larger, decorated versions. They also tend to weigh more.

Compressed peat pots are used for raising plants – such as summer bedding plants and vegetables – which are later to be planted out in the garden. The plant is never removed from the pot, so there is no root disturbance. Bituminized-paper pots are used in the same way.

Peat pellets are bought as flat peat disks and have to be soaked in water before use to expand them into 1½in (4cm) modules. They are used for propagation – a seed can be sown in each, or a cutting inserted. When the seedlings or rooted cuttings need potting, they receive no root disturbance because the peat module is potted as well.

Soil or peat blocks have the same use as peat pellets, except that you make them up at home. They are made from special "blocking mixes" and are pressed out with a special blocking tool, to form cube-shaped modules.

Seed trays

These are used for sowing seeds, for pricking out (transplanting) seedlings, and for rooting cuttings. Most are made of plastic. The standard size is 15 × 9in (38 × 23cm) and depths vary from 1 to 3in (2.5 to 7.5cm). The shallow ones are ideal for seed sowing. It's also possible to buy half-size trays for small quantities of seeds or seedlings. These are half the length of standard trays. Some plastic trays are rigid, while others (cheaper versions) are quite flexible.

There are trays available, in plastic or polystyrene, which are divided into compartments – one compartment for each seedling, cutting, or whatever. These are useful for growing summer bedding plants and vegetables which are later to be planted out, as the roots do not become entangled.

Growing bags

There has been something of a revolution in the growing of crops like tomatoes, peppers, eggplants, melons, cucumbers and lettuces. Instead of being grown in soil borders in the greenhouse, they are now frequently planted in growing bags. This means that the plants have good soil to grow in and are not at risk from soil-borne pests and diseases. If you grow in a soil border, you have to sterilize it each year to get rid of pests and diseases. And it has to be dug, manured and fertilized, with all the work and time that this entails.

Basically a growing bag is a long polyethylene bag – generally about 4ft (1.2m) long – filled with soilless mixtures. Holes are made in the top for planting. Place the bag on the greenhouse floor – if over a soil bed, first cover the bed with plastic sheeting. A 4ft (1.2m) long bag will hold four tomato, eggplant or pepper plants, or two cucumber or melon plants. Growing bags are best used only once; however, a crop of winter lettuce could be planted in them when tomatoes have finished. And then the bags should definitely be discarded – the mixture can be used on the garden.

Soil mixes

Basically there are two kinds of mixtures. One type contains soil or loam plus peat and sand, in other words a rather natural growing medium, and is generally used for seed sowing; a slightly richer mixture is used for potting seedlings and rooted cuttings; a somewhat similar mix is used for potting plants into larger pots; and still another combination is often used for plants that need a really rich mixture, as it contains a lot of fertilizer. It is used, for instance, for potting chrysanthemums into their final 8in (20cm) pots, or for large shrubs. All of these are readily available in several sizes from garden centers. Beginners are well advised to use such prepared mixes, as they are easier to manage than soilless kinds (see opposite). They do not dry out quite so quickly, and if they are allowed to dry out they are easy to moisten again. Also, the fertilizers in these mixes do not run out as quickly as they tend to do with any of the soilless combinations.

Growing bags are the modern equivalent of the greenhouse soil border. The bag should be placed on a level surface (1), and the two end flaps are normally cut off (2) to form plastic loops, which are slipped around the bag (3) to prevent it from losing its compact shape. Then most of the top of the bag is cut out (4) for planting (5). Growing bags are normally used only once, but a crop of winter lettuce, or other salad vegetable, could be planted in them when tomatoes or similar crops have finished.

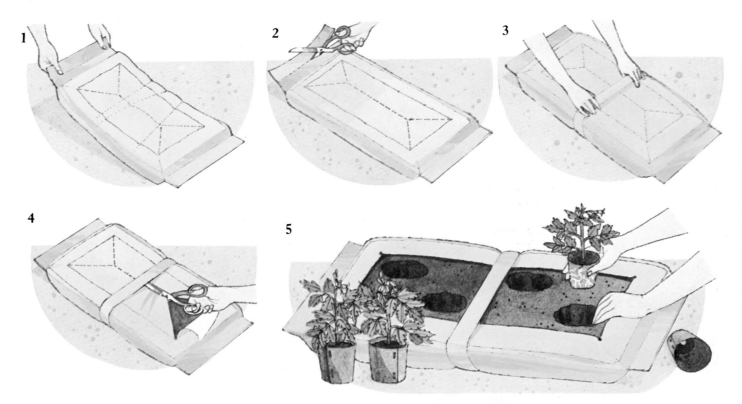

1

2

3

4

5

The other basic type of mixture is soilless – it may consist entirely of peat, or it may be a mixture of peat and sand, peat and perlite or peat and vermiculite, plus fertilizers, of course. These are inclined to dry out quickly in warm weather and if they are allowed to become really dry they are difficult to wet again.

There are available soilless seed mixtures and soilless potting mixtures. A trend now, though, is toward multipurpose mixtures, which are used for sowing seeds, rooting cuttings and for potting. Again, soilless mixtures are readily available from garden centers in various-size bags.

If you are growing lime-hating plants, such as azaleas, camellias and heathers, then make sure you buy a mixture which is free from lime or chalk – generally sold as evergreen mix.

There is no doubt that the best type of mixture for rooting cuttings is made at home – it consists of equal parts by volume of peat and coarse horticultural sand. Or you could use peat and perlite or peat and vermiculite. No fertilizers are necessary.

Greenhouse hygiene

Unless the greenhouse interior is kept scrupulously clean and tidy, all sorts of problems, mainly from pests and diseases, can occur.

Routine hygiene throughout the year consists of removing any dead and dying leaves and flowers from plants; and discarding dead and dying plants, seedlings and cuttings. If dead plant material is left the fungal disease gray mold, or botrytis, will grow on it and this will spread to healthy plants and infect them, too. Never leave any rubbish, such as heaps of dead leaves or plant remains, lying around in the greenhouse. And never store dirty pots or seed trays in the greenhouse – wash and sterilize them first.

Regular attention must be paid to controlling pests and diseases and further details will be found in Chapter Nine.

Many people are worried by green growth on the surface of mixture or soil. This may be green algae or slime, moss or liverwort. None of these primitive plants really harms cultivated plants, but if they build up

Potting and seed mixtures, whether soil or peat based, can be made at home as there are many suitable materials available like peats and sands, as well as base fertilizers. However, the newcomer to greenhouse gardening is advised to start off with ready-made proprietary mixtures.

Greenhouse smoke cones will control many pests and diseases. Some contain both insecticides and fungicides. Many gardeners use them regularly to prevent pests and diseases from gaining a foothold, but certainly light one after giving the greenhouse its annual autumn clean-up.

too much they can smother seedlings and small plants. It is therefore best to carefully scrape them off the surface and to top up with fresh mixture if necessary. Regularly stirring the surface of the mixture, very lightly, will help to stop this green growth.

Once a year, in the autumn, the greenhouse should be completely cleared of plants and thoroughly washed and sterilized. If you have permanent plants, such as greenhouse shrubs, climbers and perennials, growing in soil beds or borders then obviously these cannot be moved out, but during cleaning should be enclosed in plastic sheeting.

Use a solution of horticultural disinfectant and add a little detergent if the greenhouse is really dirty. Thoroughly scrub down everything – glass, framework, benching and even the path. You will find that green algae build up in the overlaps between the panes of glass. This can be removed by inserting a plastic plant label in the overlap between the panes and pushing it up and down.

Finish off by hosing down the structure and also direct the jet between the glass overlaps to clean them out.

The outside of the house should be washed down in the same way – it is essential to get the glass as clean as possible, for dirt on the glass cuts down the amount of light that enters the greenhouse.

If the glass is really dirty use one of the special greenhouse-glass cleaners. If green algae are a real problem in your greenhouse, growing on glass, benches, etc, then spray the structure after cleaning with one of the proprietary algicides.

Finally, before returning the plants, close down the house and burn one of the greenhouse smoke cones, containing fungicide and insecticide, to get rid of any remaining pests and diseases – although the washing down will dispose of many.

Sterilizing the greenhouse border

If you grow crops like tomatoes, peppers and eggplants in a soil border, then this must be sterilized each year after the crops have been cleared in order to kill soil-borne pests and diseases. First it should be dug and manured. Then it can be sterilized by watering it with a solution of formaldehyde. All plants must previously be removed, for the fumes from this chemical will kill them. Plants should only be returned when there is no longer any smell of fumes, and crops should not be planted in the treated border for at least six weeks.

Formaldehyde can be obtained from druggists, and it is poisonous. Dilute in water to a 2 percent solution (follow the directions on the bottle). Drench the soil with this at a rate of 5 gal per sq yd (25 l per sq m). The soil must be soaked thoroughly to a depth of at least 6in (15cm). The ventilators and door should be fully open while applying this, because heavy fumes are given off.

On completion, cover the border with a polyethylene sheet to retain the fumes and shut down the house completely. After two or three days remove the sheeting, open up the greenhouse and fork over the soil to release any remaining fumes.

Repairs and preservation

It is generally most convenient to carry out any repairs and timber-preservation treatment immediately after the annual clean-up. Obviously you would replace any broken panes of glass, but also renew any that are cracked, for these can let in drafts. Any loose putty should also be replaced to prevent drafts and leaks. Rake out the putty with an old chisel and remove any pieces of broken glass at the same time. Make sure you wear gloves to protect your hands while working.

If the greenhouse or conservatory leaks in places, then fill any holes or gaps with a silicone sealant.

A cedar greenhouse should have the framework treated regularly with a horticultural timber preservative, using cedar color. This may need doing every two years.

If the framework is soft wood, then existing paintwork should be rubbed down with sandpaper before it starts flaking, a white undercoat applied, followed by white gloss paint. Generally, paintwork should last for about three years before it needs doing again.

Cleaning containers

After use, pots and seed trays should be scrubbed clean with water to which has been added a horticultural disinfectant. This will eradicate any pests and diseases that could otherwise affect next season's planting. Dry them off and store them somewhere that is clean and dry.

Damping down

When the weather is hot and dry in the summer, you need to keep the greenhouse air humid or well charged with moisture. This is done by a technique known as

damping down. Spray the floor, staging and inside walls with plain water, once, twice, or more frequently each day, depending on weather conditions. The hotter and drier the weather, the more often you will need to damp down.

Damping down helps to prevent compost and soil drying out rapidly and to reduce the temperature, especially when done in conjunction with shading and ventilation. Do not carry out damping down during cool weather or during the autumn and winter, when the greenhouse air needs to be kept as dry as possible. The leaves of plants must also be kept dry during these periods and in cool weather.

Watering

The best time to water plants is in the morning; if it is carried out late in the day the plants and greenhouse will not dry out before nightfall and the atmosphere will be humid, favoring the development of fungal diseases. Of course, these comments do not apply when automatic watering systems are used and this is one of the disadvantages of automated watering.

If you are watering by hand, as a general rule apply water to pots or soil beds when the top ¼in (6mm) starts to dry out, ascertained by feeling the medium with your fingers. In warm weather, mixes or soil will dry out more quickly than during cool or cold conditions. Indeed, in autumn and winter, plants will need very little water. Water potted plants by completely filling the space between the mix's surface and the rim of the pot – the mixture will then be moistened right the way through.

It is best to water soil beds with a sprinkler attached to a hose. The water must penetrate to a depth of at least 6in (15cm), which means you need to apply the equivalent of 1in (2.5cm) of rain. This works out to about 5 gal per sq yd (25 l per sq m).

Soil-moisture indicators are available; these have a metal probe which is pushed into the soil and you read off the state of the soil on a calibrated dial – wet, moist or dry. Most are battery operated.

Shading and ventilating

Shading is needed in spring and summer to prevent the temperature rising too high, which can damage plants. It also prevents scorching of leaves and shriveling up of seedlings. Ideally provide shading only when the sun is shining, but this is not always possible if you are out all day, in which case shading blinds should be drawn in the morning if it is likely to be a sunny day.

Ventilation also prevents the temperature rising too high in warm weather and

Below *Insulating the greenhouse with sheets of clear plastic or bubble plastic is the major method of cutting down on fuel bills, for these materials help to hold in the heat. Plastic sheeting can also be used to partition the greenhouse if you only want to heat a small section of it, or if you want to grow cucumbers in the same house as tomatoes. The former like very humid conditions while the latter prefer an atmosphere which is drier.*

ensures plenty of fresh air. It also helps to reduce humidity and this is especially important in the autumn and winter. Ventilation is therefore needed throughout the year, consistent with maintaining minimum temperatures. When kerosene heaters are operating a little ventilation is also necessary.

Raising plants from seeds

The majority of seeds of greenhouse and bedding plants need a temperature in the region of 65–70°F (18–21°C) to germinate and are, therefore, best placed in an electrically heated propagating case after sowing. Seeds can be sown in full or half-size seed trays, or in 3½–4in (9–10cm) pots, depending on the quantity you wish to sow. Always use a proprietary seed mixture, according to instructions on the bag.

The surface of the mixture must be very smooth and level, which can be achieved by pressing with a flat piece of wood. There are various methods of sowing seeds, but you may find the following technique helpful: estimate the quantity needed for the container and hold in the palm of one hand.

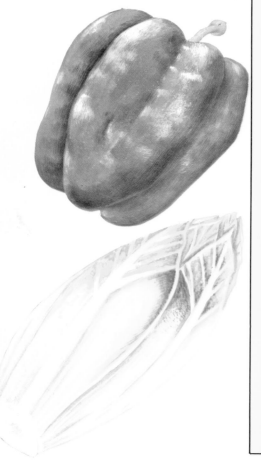

Below *Peppers may come into cropping in late spring in a warm greenhouse.*

Bottom *Belgian endive can be forced in a warm greenhouse for cutting between late winter and early spring.*

USING HEAT IN A GREENHOUSE

This table shows crops which are available in each season of the year from a greenhouse where there is gentle heat available in winter. In some cases, however, a temperature of 60°F (15.5°C) must be maintained, but the whole greenhouse need not be heated – a portion can be divided off with a temporary partition of plastic sheet, clear or black, depending on whether light is required or not. A large heated frame can be used instead in some cases, depending on the crop.

CROPPING SEASON	COLD GREENHOUSE *(Temperature not allowed to fall below freezing)*	WARM GREENHOUSE *(Minimum temperature of 60°F (15.5°C)*
Early spring	chicory*, lettuce	asparagus*, beets, carrots, endive*, green beans, lettuce, squashes, mushrooms, potatoes, radishes, rhubarb*, salad onions, strawberries
Mid-spring	asparagus*, lettuce, rhubarb*	beets, carrots, green beans, zucchini, mushrooms, potatoes, strawberries, tomatoes
Late spring	green beans, lettuce	eggplants, cucumbers, grapes, zucchini, peppers, tomatoes
Early summer	zucchini, tomatoes	eggplants, husk tomatoes, cucumbers, figs, grapes, melons, peaches, peppers
Mid-summer	eggplants, husk tomatoes, cucumbers, grapes, peaches, peppers, tomatoes	figs, melons
Late summer	eggplants, husk tomatoes, cucumbers, figs, grapes, melons, peaches, peppers, tomatoes	
Early autumn	eggplants, husk tomatoes, cucumbers, figs, green beans, grapes, melons, peaches, peppers, tomatoes	
Mid-autumn	eggplants, husk tomatoes, cucumbers, grapes, lettuce, melons, mushrooms, peppers, tomatoes	green beans
Late autumn	chicory*, lettuce	green beans, grapes, lettuce, mushrooms
Early winter	seakale*, lettuce	chicory*, endive*, lettuce, mushrooms, rhubarb*, salad onions
Midwinter	lettuce	asparagus*, chicory*, endive*, lettuce, mushrooms, radishes, rhubarb*, salad onions, seakale
Late winter	lettuce	asparagus*, beets, chicory*, endive*, lettuce, mushrooms, radishes, rhubarb*, salad onions, seakale*

*indicates crops that are lifted from the soil outdoors and brought into the greenhouse for forcing in containers or under the benches, with or without light.

The common fruit and vegetables which can be grown easily out of doors during summer are included here; the table also shows those crops which can be grown indoors as well, or can be made to crop earlier or out of season.

For the warm greenhouse crops, heat must be applied in the season during which the crop ripens, and it may also be needed for propagation in seasons which are not warm enough.

Keep in mind, however, the many and varied climates in Canada and the U.S. and adjust these tables to fit as necessary.

Hold this hand 6in (15cm) above the surface of the mixture and move it slowly from one side of the container to the other, at the same time gently tapping it with the other to allow the seeds to scatter on the surface. Seeds must be evenly spaced out and not touching each other – better to sow too thinly than too thickly. Very small seeds can be mixed with fine dry silver sand to make them easier to handle, while very large seeds can be spaced out individually. Do not cover dust-like seeds with the soil, but cover the rest with a layer equal to about twice their diameter. Sift the soil over them, using a fine sieve.

After sowing, stand the container in water until the surface becomes moist, then place in the propagating case.

When the seedlings are large enough to handle easily, they are pricked out, or transplanted, into other containers, such as seed trays, to give them room to grow. A standard-size seed tray will take 40 to 45 seedlings. Use a moderately rich potting soil for pricking out, or an equivalent soilless type.

Feeding plants

When plants are well established in their pots or beds, they should be fed on a regular basis (say every seven to fourteen days) during the spring and summer, for the fertilizer in the compost will be used up.

Most gardeners use a liquid fertilizer, diluted according to manufacturer's instructions. Use a general-purpose kind for the majority of plants, but for tomatoes, peppers and eggplants use a stronger fertilizer, and for greenhouse chrysanthemums use the same fertilizer as for tomatoes. Alternatives to liquid feeding are fertilizer tablets and spikes, inserted in the soil or mixture, or fertilizer pads placed under the pots.

Hardening off plants

Plants which are raised in a greenhouse for planting in the garden, like summer bedding plants and vegetables such as outdoor tomatoes and celery, should not be moved straight from the greenhouse to the open garden, for the change in temperature will give then a shock and check their growth. Instead, transfer them to a cold frame at least two weeks before planting-out time and subject them gradually to increased ventilation to slowly acclimatize them to outdoor conditions. This is correctly known as hardening off.

Making the most of your greenhouse

A greenhouse can be full of fruits and vegetables the year round, whether it is a cold greenhouse or heated. The accompanying tables will show you how to achieve this.

Below Melons can be grown in a heated or unheated greenhouse and cultivars should be chosen accordingly. They are not the easiest fruits to grow but nevertheless are well worth attempting.

Bottom *A rather unusual fruit, but one which is easily started in an unheated greenhouse for summer cropping, is the husk tomato, which produces little juicy fruits with a sweet to sharp taste and which can be eaten raw or cooked.*

CROP GROWING SCHEDULES

Crop growing schedules help make your greenhouse work for you with the maximum possible efficiency. Here and on the following page are four types you might try. Planned for a typical 10 × 6ft (3 × 1.8m) house, they are obviously only a guide and can easily be adapted or simplified to suit your own requirements. For example, beginners may like to start by using just part of the SALAD CROP PLAN (see page 32), following timings given for autumn-sown lettuce, tomatoes and cucumbers.

FRUIT CROP PLAN

	ON BENCHES	UNDER BENCHES		IN THE GROUND	
	Strawberries	Melons	Rhubarb	Husk tomatoes	Grapes (permanent)
Early spring		sow in heat in peat pots	crops	pot into 3in (7.5cm) pots	
Mid-spring	crops	plant in growing bags	crops	plant in ground	
Late spring	crops				
Early summer		crops			
Midsummer		crops		crops	
Late summer	plant in 6in (15cm) pots outside	crops		crops	crops
Early autumn		crops		crops	crops
Mid-autumn		crops			crops
Late autumn					
Early winter	bring into greenhouse				
Midwinter			lift and box		
Late winter		sow in heat in peat pots	lift and box	sow in heat	

LUXURY CROP PLAN

	ON BENCHES		UNDER BENCHES	
	Strawberries	**Eggplants Peppers**	**Rhubarb**	**Mushrooms**
Early spring		sow in heat	crops	
Mid-spring	crops	pot/growing bags		
Late spring	crops			
Early summer		crops		
Midsummer		crops		
Late summer	plant in 6in (15cm) pots outside	crops		spawn
Early autumn		crops		spawn
Mid-autumn				spawn; crops
Late autumn			lift and bring in	crops
Early winter	bring into greenhouse		lift and bring in	crops
Midwinter			lift and bring in; crops	
Late winter		sow in heat	crops	

Below *Ridge cucumbers, which have shorter fruit than the greenhouse varieties, may be started in a greenhouse, hardened off and planted out later. Unfortunately, the popular greenhouse cucumber is not a suitable companion for tomatoes (bottom) for it likes a very humid, steamy atmosphere, whereas tomatoes prefer drier air. The solution is to partition off the greenhouse if you want to grow both.*

SALAD CROP PLAN

	ON BENCHES			
	Green beans	**Lettuce**	**Lettuce**	**Lettuce**
Early spring		crops		
Mid-spring	crops	crops		
Late spring	crops	crops	crops	
Early summer			crops	
Midsummer				sow in bags/pots
Late summer				pot in 6in (15cm) pots
Early autumn				crops
Mid-autumn		sow in 2in (5cm) pots		crops
Late autumn		thin and plant		
Early winter				
Midwinter	sow in heat		sow	
Late winter			sow in heat	

ALL YEAR ROUND PLAN

	ON BENCHES			
	Lettuce	**Potatoes**	**Melons**	**Cucumbers**
Early spring			sow in heat in pots	pot
Mid-spring		crops	plant in growing bags	plant
Late spring		crops	plant in growing bags	
Early summer			crops	crops
Midsummer			crops	crops
Late summer	sow in pots		crops	crops
Early autumn	sow in pots		crops	crops
Mid-autumn	sow in pots		crops	crops
Late autumn				
Early winter	crops			
Midwinter	crops	plant in heat		
Late winter	crops		sow in heat in pots	sow in heat

IN THE GROUND

Tomatoes	Lettuce	Lettuce	Asparagus	Melons	Grapes (permanent)
			crops		
crops			crops		
crops					
crops				sow	
				sow	crops
	sow	sow		plant	crops
	crops	sow			
	crops			60°F (15.5°C)	crops
		crops	lift and box	crops	crops
sow		crops	lift and box	crops	
3in (7.5cm) pots		crops	lift and box		
plant			crops		

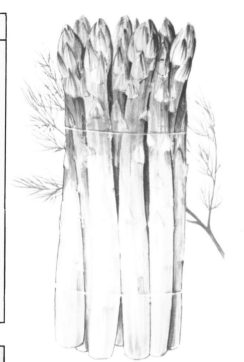

IN THE GROUND

Salad onions	Cucumbers	Radishes	Tomatoes	Radishes	Carrots or Beets
sow in heat	sow in heat		prick out	sow; crops	crops
	prick out		plant	crops	crops
crops	plant		plant		
			crops		
	crops		crops		
	crops		crops		
	crops	sow; crops	crops		
	crops	sow; crops	crops		
		crops	crops		
		crops			
					sow in heat
			sow in heat		sow in heat

UNDER BENCHES		IN THE GROUND			
Rhubarb	Mushrooms	Tomatoes	Lettuce	Carrots or Beets	Radishes
crops		plant			
crops					
		crops			
		crops			
		plant	sow		
	spawn	plant	sow		
	spawn	crops			
	spawn	crops	crops		
	spawn; crops	crops	crops	sow in heat	
	crops	crops			sow in heat
lift and box	crops	sow in heat		crops	sow in heat; crops
lift and box		pot		crops	crops

Top *Asparagus is a luxury crop for forcing in a cool or warm greenhouse. Roots are lifted from the garden in autumn, boxed up and forced for winter or spring harvesting.*

Above *Tasty young forcing carrots can be pulled in winter if sowings are made in the greenhouse during autumn. Heat is needed for this out of season crop.*

CHAPTER 5
ORNAMENTAL PLANTS TO GROW

Keeping your greenhouse full of flowers all year round is easy to do, provided you keep it frost free. And even the smallest greenhouse should provide pot plants and cut flowers to brighten up your home, at a fraction of their store-bought cost.

Alpines

These are rock-garden plants which can be grown in special, shallow pots – or pans – and flowered in an unheated greenhouse in winter and spring. Examples are gentians, alpine primroses and saxifrages, but there are many more.

Buy young plants in autumn and plant in 6in (15cm) diameter clay or plastic pans or half-pots. Use a not-too-rich potting mixture, to which has been added one-third extra of coarse grit.

For most of the year the plants are kept in cold frames, with the covers on, but well ventilated, only in autumn and winter. Plants are transferred to a greenhouse as they are coming into flower.

Annuals, hardy

Hardy annuals, such as clarkia, cornflower, godetia and lavatera, can be flowered in the spring in pots in an unheated or cool greenhouse, if sown in late summer or early autumn. Germinate seed in a cold frame and prick off seedlings into 3½in (9cm) pots. Pot on into 5in (12.5cm) pots. Grow in a cold frame until early winter, then transfer to the greenhouse. Use a soil-based mixture for sowing and growing. Keep only slightly moist in winter, provide maximum light and good ventilation. Water and feed well when plants are actively growing and flowering.

African daisy

African daisies *(Gerbera)* are perennial plants with large, daisy-like flowers, in many colors, in spring and summer. They need a minimum temperature of 45°F (7°C), and are best grown in soil-based mixture. They need plenty of ventilation, good light, but shade from strong sun, and the soil mix should be kept only slightly moist. It is now possible to raise plants from seeds, and if these are sown in mid- or late winter they will flower the same year, as modern strains are very quick to mature.

Begonia, tuberous

The tuberous begonias have large, double flowers in many brilliant colors and flower in summer. They need a minimum temperature of 55°F (13°C).

In late winter or early spring, place the tubers in moist peat and start them into growth in a temperature of 65°F (18°C). Pot into 5in (12.5cm) pots when the shoots have formed. Use soilless or soil-based mixture. Shade from strong sun and water as needed. Feed regularly when buds start to develop. After flowering, reduce watering gradually until the soil mix is dry and the stems have died down. Remove the tubers from pots and store in dry peat in a frost-proof place.

Bird of paradise flower

This is a large perennial plant *(Strelitzia reginae)*, with spectacular orange and blue flowers, resembling a bird's head, in summer. It is easily grown in a minimum temperature of 45°F (7°C), and has attractive leathery, evergreen leaves.

Pot on young plants in spring until

Right *The tuberous begonias are favorite summer-flowering pot plants with their double, often exceedingly large flowers. Some cultivars are pendulous in habit (as shown here) and make very fine subjects for hanging baskets or for trailing over the edge of the benches.*

Far right *The hippeastrum, or amaryllis, is a bulbous plant for a heated greenhouse, producing huge blooms in winter or spring. Red is a favorite color, but also available are pinks, whites and bicolor cultivars.*

There are few easier and more colorful subjects for spring flowering in an unheated greenhouse than the hardy dwarf bulbs. There are many to choose from, including the popular snowdrop. Ideally this should be potted as soon as flowering is over, while the leaves are still green, as then establishment and subsequent flowering is very much more successful.

eventually they are in a large tub or pot; or they can be grown in a soil bed in a conservatory. Plenty of sun and good ventilation are needed; keep only slightly moist in winter. Feed well in summer for steady growth. Use soilless or soil-based mixture.

Brunfelsia

This easily grown evergreen shrub is suitable for an average-size greenhouse. Large, blue-purple flowers are produced in summer. The minimum temperature needed is 50°F (10°C).

Young plants should be potted on as required in spring, or can be grown in a soil bed in the conservatory. Use soil-based potting mixture. Pinch out the growing tips of young plants to create bushy specimens. Water as required, feed in summer and shade from strong sun. Pruning is not generally needed.

Bulbs, dwarf hardy

Hardy dwarf bulbs can be grown in pots to flower in an unheated greenhouse in spring, making good companions for alpines. Examples are crocus species, glory of the snow *(Chionodoxa),* winter aconites *(Eranthis),* snowdrops *(Galanthus),* grape hyacinths *(Muscari),* miniature daffodils *(Narcissus),* squills *(Scilla)* and dwarf tulip species.

Grow in 6in (15cm) diameter pans or half-pots. Use soil-based mixture. Pot in early autumn, about 1in (2.5cm) apart each way. Keep in a well-ventilated cold frame until

late autumn. After flowering return to the frame and water till leaves have died down.

Bulbs, hardy

The large-flowering daffodils, hyacinths, tulips and crocuses can be flowered in pots during winter and spring in a cold or slightly heated greenhouse.

Bulbs are planted in late autumn, generally in 6in (15cm) diameter bowls or pans. Bulb fiber can be used, or soilless mixture. Keep bulbs cool and dark after planting, e.g. by plunging them 6in (15cm) deep in weathered ashes or sand in a cool shaded place outdoors. When the bulbs have produced shoots (five to eight weeks) transfer to the greenhouse. After flowering, they should be planted in the garden.

Busy Lizzies

Busy Lizzies *(Impatiens)* make good pot plants for summer flowering, after which they are discarded. Modern strains, which are raised from seeds sown in early or mid-spring, are neat, compact, free-flowering plants in a wide range of colors. A minimum temperature of 50°F (10°C) is needed.

They can be flowered in 5in (12.5cm) pots and soilless mixtures are particularly suitable. Provide light shade, high humidity and water freely. Take cuttings in summer.

Cacti

There is a wide range to choose from, but those which flower freely and regularly include the peanut cactus *(Chamaecereus),* mammillarias and rebutias. Most will survive with a minimum temperature of 40°F (4.5°C).

Provide maximum light and sun – there is no need to shade them – good ventilation and a dry atmosphere. Keep the soil mix dry between late autumn and mid-spring and water normally for the rest of the year. Pot on as necessary, using a proprietary cactus compost. Spring is the best time for potting.

Camellias

These are evergreen shrubs with pink, red or white flowers in winter or spring. They can be flowered in an unheated or cool greenhouse or conservatory and are best grown in tubs or large pots, using lime-free or evergreen mix.

Put the plants under glass in autumn, give good ventilation and make sure the compost remains steadily moist. After flowering, the plants can be stood outdoors in a sheltered, partially shaded spot. Never let the compost dry out, and remember to feed regularly with a liquid fertilizer during the summer months.

Cape primrose

The Cape primroses *(Streptocarpus)* are perennials which produce tubular flowers in the summer in various colors. A minimum temperature of 45°F (7°C) is needed.

They can be raised from seeds sown in early spring. High humidity is appreciated in summer, together with shade from strong sun. Water regularly in spring and summer, but give the plants a rest in autumn and winter by keeping them only barely moist and cool. Plants can be propagated from leaf cuttings in summer.

Carnations

Perpetual-flowering carnations *(Dianthus)* are capable of blooming all year round, if sufficient heat is available. For flower production in winter a minimum temperature of 50°F (10°C) is needed. With a winter temperature of 40°F (4.5°C), blooms will be pro-duced for most of the year except winter.

Provide maximum light all year round, good ventilation and a dry atmosphere in winter. Plants are bought from specialist growers, are grown in soil-based mixture and eventually need a pot size of at least 6in (15cm). For large blooms, pinch out the small side buds situated around the central or main flower bud.

Chilean bellflower

This is a climber *(Lapageria rosea)* suitable for a conservatory with a minimum temperature of 40°F (4.5°C). Large, waxy, tubular, deep-pink blooms are produced in late summer and autumn.

It is best planted in a soil bed but can be grown in a large pot of soilless mixture. In summer give good ventilation and light shading. The only pruning needed is thinning out weak stems in spring.

Although most are hardy shrubs, camellias can be flowered in an unheated or cool greenhouse. They are superb plants for the conservatory. Plants are best grown in tubs so that they can be moved outdoors after flowering. Most popular are the many cultivars of Camellia japonica.

Chrysanthemums

Late-flowering chrysanthemums bloom in the autumn and early winter, when they need a small amount of artificial heat – just enough (coupled with ventilation) to keep the atmosphere dry. They are flowered in 8in (20cm) pots and young plants are progressively potted on to these from early spring. Use a fairly rich potting soil for the final potting.

The plants are stood outdoors from early summer until early autumn, when they are returned to the greenhouse. Pinch out tips of young plants in spring to encourage branching. Allow the central flower bud on each stem to develop and remove all the surrounding small ones. Feed and water well in summer.

Cineraria

These flower in late winter and spring, producing heads of daisy-like flowers in many colors. These pot plants are raised from seeds between mid-spring and early summer and discarded after flowering. Provide a minimum temperature of 45°F (7°C).

Final pot size is 5in (12.5cm). Keep plants in a cold frame for the summer, well ventilated, shaded, and with steadily moist soil mix. Move into the greenhouse in early autumn. The greenhouse should be well ventilated, the leaves must be kept dry and the soil mix not allowed to become wet.

Cyclamen

These pot plants grow from tubers and bloom in autumn and winter. A minimum temperature of 50°F (10°C) is needed.

Seeds are sown in late summer for flowering the following year. Final-size pots are 5in (12.5cm) and soilless mixture is suitable. Cool, well-ventilated conditions should be provided at all times. Plants can be kept in a shady cold frame in the second summer and re-housed in early autumn. Dry off and rest the tubers after flowering. Re-start into growth in late summer by re-potting in fresh potting mix and watering.

Flame nettle

The flame nettle (Coleus) is a short-term pot plant grown for its brightly colored foliage. Often this is marked with various colors. Minimum temperature needed is 50°F (10°).

Sow seeds in spring and pot on young plants until they are in 5in (12.5cm) pots. Use soilless or soil-based mixture. Good light is needed and high humidity in warm weather. Pinch out tips of young plants to create bushy specimens. Feed and water well in summer. Discard old plants in autumn, as they become leggy.

Freesias

These are grown from corms and produce scented flowers in a wide range of colors during winter. Provide a minimum temperature of 45°F (7°C).

Plant corms in late summer – eight to a 6in (15cm) pot, using soil-based mixture. Place in cold frame and cover with peat. Transfer to greenhouse after six weeks. Give good ventilation and water moderately. Dry off the corms after flowering and re-pot and start into growth again in late summer. Freesias can also be raised from seeds, sown in late winter or early spring.

Fuchsia

This is the most popular summer-flowering pot plant, with attractive flowers in a wide range of colors. It is an ideal plant for the cool greenhouse.

Buy in young plants in spring and pot on until they are in 6in (15cm) pots. Soilless mixture is particularly suitable. Provide good ventilation and shade from strong sun throughout the summer. Keep the mixture steadily moist. Pinch out their growing tips to encourage branching.

Feed weekly in summer. To produce new plants, take cuttings in early summer. The resultant young plants should be overwintered in a minimum temperature of 50°F (10°C). Old plants, if kept, should be rested over winter by keeping the soil mix dry. Plants will then drop their leaves. For old plants, a temperature of 40°F (4.5°C) is adequate over winter.

Gloxinia

Gloxinias (Sinningia) grow from tubers and produce large, bell-shaped blooms in summer in various colors. A minimum temperature of 60°F (15.5°C) is needed.

Pot tubers in spring, using soil-based or soilless mixture: one per 5in (12.5cm) pot. Provide a temperature of 70°F (21°C) to start the tubers into growth. Provide shade and high humidity during summer and feed weekly. Dry off the tubers at the end of the season and store them in the pots in a frost-free greenhouse.

Hippeastrum

This bulbous plant, often called amaryllis, produces large, trumpet-shaped blooms in winter or spring. A minimum temperature of 50°F (10°C) is needed.

Pot one bulb per 6in (15cm) pot, using soil-based pot mix, and leave the upper part of the bulb exposed. Start into growth in late winter. After flowering, feed weekly; in late summer, when the leaves die down, drastically reduce watering, keeping the pot mix barely moist, to give the plants a rest. Start into growth again in late winter.

Below *Although cyclamen are often discarded after flowering, they can be kept for a number of years as they grow from a tuber. Eventually they make large plants with dozens of flowers.*

Far right *The late-flowering chrysanthemums are among the most popular of flowering plants for the unheated or slightly heated greenhouse. They are easily grown, in large pots, and spend the summer out of doors. Most gardeners use the blooms for cutting.*

Although it produces exotic-looking blooms, the blue passion flower is nevertheless an easily grown climber for the cool greenhouse or conservatory. It is a vigorous plant and will need regular pruning to keep it within bounds.

Hydrangeas

These produce large, mop-like blooms, pink or blue, in the spring. Provide a minimum temperature of 45°F (7°C).

Young plants should be potted on in spring and summer until they are in 6in (45cm) pots. Use an acid soil mix if blue flowers are required. Grow in a cold frame for the summer and re-house in early autumn. Keep the soil mix only just moist in winter. After flowering, the plants can be placed outdoors for the summer. New plants can be raised easily from cuttings taken in mid- or late spring.

Ivies

The ivies *(Hedera)* can be used as climbers or trailers. Some have plain green leaves while others are variegated. They are hardy so can be grown in an unheated greenhouse, but they are also suitable for a cool house.

The green-leaved kinds are ideal for shady parts of the greenhouse, such as under the benches, while variegated kinds need good light to maintain their color. Shade from strong sun, though. Provide high humidity during warm weather. Feed in the growing season, and keep much drier in the winter months.

Paper flower

The paper flower *(Bougainvillea)* is a colorful climber for the heated conservatory – minimum temperature 50°F (10°C). Modified leaves, or bracts, around the flowers provide the color – purple, red, magenta, crimson or orange.

The plant needs plenty of sun, good ventilation and high humidity in summer. Keep much drier in winter. Water well in summer. In early spring, cut out weak shoots and leave the strong stems. Reduce these by one-third if desired. Grow in a soil bed or large pot or tub.

Passion flower

The blue passion flower *(Passiflora caerulea)* is an easy climber for the conservatory with a minimum temperature of 50°F (10°C).

The passion flower needs humidity and light shade in warm weather, normal watering, but keep much drier in winter. Prune in early spring by thinning out some of the stems, if growth becomes congested. Take out the oldest and leave the younger ones. Cut back side shoots on those remaining to 6in (15cm).

Pelargonium

The regal pelargonium is a popular perennial plant for summer flowering in the heated greenhouse – a minimum winter temperature of 50°F (10°C) is needed. Its flowers are available in many colors.

Grow the plants in 5in (12.5cm) pots of soil-based mixture. Good light is needed and adequate sun, but shade from very strong sunshine. A dry atmosphere is needed all through the year, plus good ventilation. Water as needed in summer, but keep only just moist in winter. Raise new plants from cuttings in late summer – old plants are best discarded.

Poor man's orchid

Poor man's orchid *(Schizanthus)* is a slightly tender annual and needs a minimum temperature of 45–50°F (7–10°C). It has orchid-like blooms in bright color combinations and these are produced in winter or spring.

Seeds are sown in late summer and germinated in a cold frame. Grow young plants in a cold frame and pot on until final 6in (15cm) pots are reached. Take the plants into the greenhouse in early autumn and provide well-ventilated conditions. Do not allow the compost to become very wet.

Primroses

Three kinds of primroses or primula are generally grown – *Primula malacoides, P. obconica* (both in various colors), and the yellow *P. × kewensis.* They flower in winter and spring and need a minimum tempera-

ture of 45°F (7°C). Sow seeds any time between late winter and late spring.

Pot on young plants until 5in (12.5cm) pots are reached. Grow in a cold frame from early summer to early autumn, shade from strong sun and keep moist. In the greenhouse, ensure good light, plenty of ventilation, and keep the soil mix steadily moist, but do not wet the foliage. Discard after flowering.

Slipperwort

The slipperwort *(Calceolaria)* is a popular pot plant for spring flowering, after which it is discarded. It has large pouched flowers in a wide range of brilliant colors. A minimum temperature of 45°F (7°C) is needed.

Sow seeds in early summer and pot on young plants until they are in 5in (12.5cm) pots. Grow cool at all times – they hate high temperatures. Grow young plants in a cold frame and take into the greenhouse in mid-autumn. Good light is needed and plenty of ventilation. Make sure the soil mix is not kept wet in autumn or winter.

Wax flower

The wax flower *(Hoya carnosa)* is an evergreen climber with clusters of white waxy flowers produced between late spring and autumn. It is ideal for the small greenhouse or conservatory, grown in a pot or in the greenhouse border. The minimum temperature needed is 45°F (7°C).

In summer, provide humidity and light shade from strong sun; water as required but keep barely moist in winter. Liquid feed during the summer. Pruning is not generally needed, and the long stems are often trained around circular wire frames.

Winter cherry

In autumn and winter, the winter cherry *(Solanum capsicastrum)* and Jerusalem or Christmas cherry *(S. pseudocapsicum)* produce orange or red berries. Plants are usually discarded when the display is over. A minimum temperature of 45°F (7°C) is needed.

Sow seeds in late winter or early spring. Young plants are potted on until they are in 5in (12.5cm) pots.

Pinch out the tips of young plants to encourage branching. Place out of doors for the summer. When the plants are in flower, spray them daily with plain water to ensure a good set of berries. Move into the greenhouse in early autumn and provide good ventilation.

Slipperworts, with their brilliant pouched flowers in spring, need to be kept as cool as possible, so are ideal short-term pot plants where minimum artificial heat is provided. They are raised from seeds sown in early summer.

CHAPTER 6
VEGETABLES TO GROW

There are few aspects of greenhouse gardening more rewarding than growing your own vegetables. The range of crops you can grow is enormous, and you can also use your greenhouse to give a head start to vegetables for planting out in spring.

Below *It is possible to produce early beet crops in spring in a cold or slightly heated greenhouse, and the roots are harvested when about the size of a golf ball. Bottom: Eggplants are as easy to grow as tomatoes and indeed make ideal companion crops as they need the same conditions. Most gardeners aim to produce a summer crop.*

Far right *Although cucumbers are easy to grow if warm, very humid conditions can be provided, they are not suitable for combining with tomatoes, eggplants or peppers; however, part of the greenhouse could be screened off for cucumbers.*

Asparagus
For out-of-season asparagus, from mid-winter onward, lift four-year-old crowns, which have not been cut from previously, in late autumn, after the foliage has died down. Leave plenty of soil around the roots. Store the crowns in a cold, dark place for about a week. Plant the crowns close together under the benches in boxes 9in (23cm) deep, covering them with 4in (10cm) sifted soil. Maintain a temperature of 60°F (15.5°C) and a steady supply of moisture. They should be ready for cutting three weeks later.

Eggplants
Eggplants, or aubergines, are becoming quite popular with gardeners. Because they are grown in a similar way to tomatoes, and need the same conditions, these two crops can be grown successfully together.

Basic conditions needed are good light but shade from strong sunshine; plenty of ventilation; and a temperature of 60–70°F (15.5–21°C), with a minimum of 55°F (13°C) at night. It is a summer crop, but some artificial heat will be needed in the early part of the year.

The usual time to sow seeds is in early spring. As the seeds are large, they can be spaced out 1in (2.5cm) apart on the surface of seed mixture. Use a seed tray and a soil-based mixture. A temperature of 60–65°F (15.5–18°C) is needed for germination.

Seedlings are transplanted (pricked out) individually into 3in (7.5cm) pots, and then moved on into 5in (12.5cm) pots. For both stages use a soil-based potting mixture. The tips of the young plants should be pinched out when a height of 6in (15cm) has been reached as this results in bushy plants and, therefore, more fruits.

Plant in a soil border, growing bags or large pots, when the plants are about 6in (15cm) in height. Bamboo canes or growing bag crop supports will be needed. For details of planting see TOMATOES.

When the flowers are open, gently tap their stems to pollinate the flowers and ensure a good set of fruits. When some fruits have set, give weekly liquid feed.

Beets
Early beets are easy to produce in a cold or slightly heated greenhouse, using cultivars of round-rooted beet. They can be harvested when about the size of a golf ball.

The beets can be grown in a soil border but make sure it has not been freshly manured or this may result in over sized roots. Growing bags can also be used.

Sow the seeds thinly in early spring, in seed drills 1in (2.5cm) deep, and spaced about 6in (15cm) apart. When the seedlings are large enough to handle, thin them out to 2–3in (5–7.5cm) apart. This may seem close, but the roots are gathered when small.

Keep the soil steadily moist (not wet) and provide good light and ventilation. You should be able to start harvesting about eight weeks after sowing.

Carrots
It is possible to obtain really early carrots by growing stump-rooted forcing cultivars in a greenhouse. For the earliest crops try to provide a temperature of about 50°F (10°C), although good results can also be obtained in an unheated or very cool greenhouse.

Sowings can be made in autumn or in mid- to late winter. Ideally, sow in a soil border, but growing bags can be used. The soil must not be freshly manured or this will result in oversized roots.

Sow the seeds in drills about ½in (12mm) deep and spaced 4in (10cm) apart. Thin out the seedlings as necessary to stand about 1in (2.5cm) apart.

Carrots must have very good light and ventilation, and the soil should be kept steadily moist. Roots can be pulled as soon as they are large enough to use; pencil-thickness is fine for these delicious, out-of-season crops.

Cucumbers
This popular crop needs a very humid atmosphere, and a temperature of 65–70°F (18–21°C), with a minimum of 60°F (15.5°C) at night. It will be necessary to provide artificial heat in the early part of the year.

Cucumbers are not suitable for growing with tomatoes, eggplants or peppers,

because they need much higher humidity. However, part of the greenhouse could be screened off for the cucumbers, with a sheet of clear polyethylene.

Many of the cultivars listed in catalogs are F_1 hybrids: these are not as easy to grow as ordinary cultivars, so choose the latter if you do not have much experience.

The normal sowing period is early to mid-spring. Use 3in (7.5cm) pots and soilless mixture. Sow one seed per pot, pushing it, on edge, into the mixture. Provide a germination temperature of 65–75°F (18–24°C).

When young plants have produced their first true leaves, plant in a well-manured soil border, in growing bags (two plants per bag), or in 9in (22.5cm) pots (use a rich potting soil mix). When planting in a soil border, set each plant on a mound of a good, fairly rich potting soil.

The top of the root-ball must be ½in (12mm) above the soil or soil mix to make sure water does not collect around the base of the stem, which would cause rotting. Plants are spaced 24in (60cm) apart.

The plants must be trained along horizontal wires, 12in (30cm) apart along one side of the greenhouse. The main stem is tied in to these, and the tip pinched out when the top wire is reached. Side shoots must be pinched out at two leaves beyond a female flower (this has a small fruit behind it) and tied to the wires. Tendrils should be removed. Some cultivars produce male and female flowers, others (mainly the F_1 hybrids) only females. Male flowers may be removed before they open (these are the ones with only a thin stalk behind them).

The greenhouse should be damped down twice a day; in warm weather spray plants with plain water twice daily. Provide light shade from hot sunshine. From six weeks after planting, feed once a week with a general-purpose liquid fertilizer. The soil must be kept constantly moist.

White roots will eventually appear on the surface of the soil mix – top-dress them with 1in (2.5cm) of similar soil mix. This must not touch the stems, though. Harvest fruits when large enough to use.

Green beans

For the earliest crops of green beans, try growing them under glass. It can be unheated or just frost free. The climbing cultivars are recommended, as they produce a heavier crop than the dwarf kinds.

Seeds can be sown at various times – in early spring if you can provide heat; otherwise in mid- to late spring. For a really early crop, a sowing can be made in midwinter if you can maintain a minimum temperature of 50°F (10°C).

Use 3½in (9cm) pots and soil-based mixture. Sow one seed per pot. The young plants are planted in a row, 12in (30cm) apart. The stems are trained up strings fixed to a strong horizontal wire in the roof of the greenhouse. The bottom of each string can be secured at soil level with a wooden or wire peg.

The plants must be provided with good light and ventilation and the soil kept constantly moist. You should be able to start picking beans from late spring onward.

Chicory or curly endives

This is a salad crop, rather like lettuce, and is grown for winter use in a cool or unheated greenhouse. The type to grow is the broad-leaved escarole.

Seeds are sown in late summer. They may be sown direct in a soil border, or in containers, and the seedlings transplanted. See LETTUCES for further details of plant raising.

Chicory likes a fertile soil, so grow in a well-manured soil bed or in growing bags. Plants should be spaced 12in (30cm) apart each way. Provide the same conditions as for lettuces.

The leaves of chicory can be rather bitter unless they are blanched. To blanch, each plant is covered with a large flower pot, with the hole plugged to exclude light, several weeks before harvesting. Do not begin blanching until the chicory are fully grown.

Lettuces

Lettuces can be harvested under glass from mid-autumn to mid- or late spring, depending on sowing times and cultivars grown. There are cultivars suited to unheated and heated greenhouses, and it is important to choose cultivars for your particular conditions.

Sowing time depends on the cultivars chosen, but is between late summer and midwinter. It is best to sow a small amount of seed of each cultivar in a 3½in (9cm) pot, using soil-based or soilless seed mixture. The seeds should be germinated in a temperature of 50–60°F (10–15.5°C): no higher or the seeds may not grow. As soon as large enough to handle, transplant seedlings individually into small peat pots or soil blocks.

Lettuces can be grown in a soil border, which should have been dug and manured for a previous crop, such as tomatoes. Rake in a general-purpose fertilizer before planting. Lettuces should be planted 8in (20cm) apart each way. Do not plant too deeply; the lower leaves should be just clear of the surface. Growing bags can also be used for lettuces, including those which previously contained a crop of tomatoes, peppers, eggplants, etc, in the summer.

Far left *Use the climbing varieties of green beans for growing in a cold or frost-free greenhouse, for they bear heavier crops than the dwarf varieties. Depending on the amount of heat available, beans can be ready for picking in spring or early summer.*

Below *There are many varieties of lettuce for growing under glass, to provide salad material between mid-autumn and late spring. Most are suitable for unheated greenhouses but a few need some artificial heat.*

Far right *Sweet peppers or capsicums are as easy to grow as tomatoes. The fruits can be picked when they are green or unripe, or when fully ripe, when they will be red or yellow, depending on variety.*

Lettuces must have maximum light and really good ventilation. The greenhouse air must be kept dry: if it is damp the fungal disease gray mold, or botrytis, will attack the plants and cause them to rot. The soil must be kept reasonably moist, but when watering try not to wet the leaves.

Lettuces can be harvested when you consider they are a suitable size, but bear in mind that most greenhouse cultivars do not produce the large solid hearts which are typical of some outdoor lettuces.

Mushrooms

An easy way for the greenhouse gardener to grow mushrooms is to buy one of the proprietary mushroom kits. These can be obtained from garden centers.

These kits or packs are very often supplied in a special plastic bag or plastic tub, which contains the compost, and generally they are ready to start into growth – just follow the simple instructions supplied.

Mushrooms like a reasonably high temperature, 50–60°F (10–15.5°C) being ideal. If you cannot maintain this during the colder months of the year, then make a start as the weather warms up in the spring, and continue growing throughout summer and into early autumn. Contrary to popular belief, it is not necessary to grow mushrooms in completely dark conditions, but a convenient place for your mushroom kit would be under the greenhouse bench. You can expect several "flushes" or crops of mushrooms from the proprietary kits, and they should be harvested while small. Twist them out of the compost rather than cutting the stalks.

Peppers

Sweet peppers, or capsicums, are becoming almost as popular as tomatoes and they also crop during the summer. They make good companions for tomatoes as they require the same conditions: dryish air, warmth and a good amount of sunshine. An ideal temperature range is 60–70°F (15.5–21°C), with a minimum at night of 55°F (13°C). Artificial heat will be needed in the early part of the year.

Seeds are usually sown in early spring, although you can sow from midwinter onward if sufficient heat is available. Use a seed tray and a soil-based mixture, and space out the seeds 1in (2.5cm) apart each way. The recommended germination temperature is 65°F (18°C). When the seedlings are large enough to handle easily, prick them out individually into 3in (7.5cm) pots, using a soil-based potting mixture. Before they outgrow these, pot on into 5in (12.5cm) pots. Pinch out the tips of plants when 6in (15cm) high to ensure bushy plants and therefore more peppers.

For details of planting peppers, see TOMATOES. Set the plants 18in (45cm) apart each way. Grow in the soil bed, growing bags or in 10–12in (25–30cm) pots. Plant out when 6in (15cm) high. The plants will need supports – bamboo canes or growing-bag crop supports.

When the flowers have opened, gently tap the flower stems to pollinate the flowers and so ensure fruit setting. Keep the soil or soil mix steadily moist, ventilate well in warm weather and shade from strong sunshine.

When the first fruits have set, start weekly feeding, using a liquid tomato fertilizer.

The fruits can be picked and used when they are green or unripe, or they can be left until they are fully ripe, when they will be red or yellow, according to cultivar.

Potatoes

If you are maintaining a heated greenhouse, try growing some really early potatoes – to harvest in mid-spring. A temperature of 50°F (10°C) is needed. You can also have new potatoes in time for Christmas if you plant them in early autumn and supply sufficient heat.

To harvest in mid-spring, plant tubers or "seed potatoes" in midwinter. First, though, you need to sprout or chit them –

that is, encourage shoots to grow. Place the tubers in a seed tray – the end where the dormant buds are situated should face upward. Keep them in a frost-proof place with plenty of light and air. When the shoots are about ½in (12mm) long the tubers can be planted.

Potatoes can be grown in large pots. Plant three tubers per 8in (20cm) pot, or five in a 12in (30cm) pot. Growing bags can also be used and a 4ft (1.2m) long bag will hold about eight tubers.

When planting in pots, half fill each with a rich, soil-based potting mixture, set the tubers an equal distance apart and cover with 2in (5cm) of the mix. Water well and place on the floor of the greenhouse or on the benches. It is necessary to ensure maximum light.

More soil mix should be added to the pots as the shoots grow, so that the tips are only just showing. Eventually the soil mix level should be 1in (2.5cm) below the rim of the pot.

If planting in growing bags, set the tubers about 3in (7.5cm) deep.

Keep the soil mix steadily moist and feed with a general-purpose liquid fertilizer once there is a lot of top growth.

Early cultivars of potato should be chosen for these early crops.

Radishes

In a greenhouse heated to about 50°F (10°C), it is possible to harvest radishes in autumn and winter. Radishes are very quick maturing and those cultivars specially bred for forcing or for early cropping should be chosen.

Sowings can be started in autumn and continued in succession throughout the winter.

Grow in a soil bed, but not freshly manured, or in growing bags. Sow the seeds thinly, as the rate of germination is usually very high. Rows should be spaced 4in (10cm) apart. If necessary, thin the seedlings to 1in (2.5cm) apart. Really good light is needed, plus generous ventilation. It is essential to keep the soil moist at all times – if allowed to dry out, growth will slow down and roots will be hard and woody.

Salad onions

These are a good crop to grow with radishes for winter supplies. Again a temperature of 50°F (10°C) is needed, plus good light and ventilation.

Seeds can be sown in early autumn in a soil bed, growing bags or even large pots. In a soil bed, rows are spaced 6in (15cm) apart. Sow fairly thickly and pull as soon as large enough for use. The soil must be kept steadily moist.

Tomatoes

Tomatoes are a most popular crop at any time, whether they are grown indoors or out. The recommended temperature is 60–70°F (15.5–21°C), with a minimum at night of 55°F (13°C). Do not allow the temperature to fall any lower or growth will slow down or stop. Artificial heat will be necessary in the early part of the year. Try to maintain a dryish atmosphere.

For summer crops, sow seeds in early spring, using a seed tray and soil-based seed mixture. The seeds are large enough to be spaced out 1in (2.5cm) apart each way. Provide a temperature of 65°F (18°C) for germination. When the seedlings are large enough to handle easily, transplant them individually to 3in (7.5cm) pots, using soil-based potting mixture. Before the plants outgrow these, pot on into 5in (12.5cm) pots.

When the plants are 6in (15cm) high they are planted out. If you have an unheated greenhouse, it would be advisable to buy plants, and to plant them in late spring.

Whatever method of growing is used, tomato plants should be at least 18in (45cm) apart each way. They can be grown in a soil border, well dug and manured in the previous autumn. Apply a general-purpose fertilizer before planting.

Growing bags may also be used for raising tomatoes – if they are to be placed on a soil bed, first cover the soil with a sheet of polyethylene. A 4ft (1.2m) long bag will hold three plants.

Tomatoes can also be grown in 10–12in (25–30cm) pots, using a rich soil-based potting mixture. Again, if they are to be placed on soil, first lay a sheet of plastic.

Provide supports after planting – 6ft (1.8m) bamboo canes or growing-bag crop supports. Tie in the plants regularly as they grow. Rub out side shoots as they appear, so the tomato is trained as a single stem.

The soil or mixture must be kept steadily moist – do not allow it to dry out or become very wet. Ideally, use water of moderate temperature. Ventilate well and shade lightly from very strong sunshine.

Flowers should be pollinated when fully open by gently tapping the flower stems. This will ensure a good set of fruit. Feed weekly, using a liquid tomato fertilizer, as soon as the first fruits have formed.

When five or six trusses of flowers have been produced, pinch out the tip of each plant to prevent further upward growth.

A few of the lower leaves can be removed as soon as the lower fruits start to ripen to ensure good air circulation around the fruits. Do not cut off too many leaves, though, as this may prevent or retard the development of the young fruits.

Below *If a minimum temperature of 50°F (10°C) can be provided, salad onions can be grown for pulling in the winter. Seeds are sown quite thickly in early autumn in any suitable container or in a soil bed.*

Far right *Tomatoes can be a major crop in amateur greenhouses and most people will aim for an early harvest. Clearly out-of-season crops are possible if sufficient heat can be provided. Today there are many varieties available, including yellow and orange ones, and the large beefsteak kinds.*

CHAPTER 7

FRUIT TO GROW

Luxury fruit – peaches, figs and grapes, for example – are expensive to buy in the shops, and their flavor can be disappointing. Use your greenhouse to grow luxury fruit to perfection, out of season.

Figs

The fig is a large vigorous tree and when grown under glass growth needs to be severely restricted. This is best achieved by growing the trees in 10–12in (25–30cm) pots, to restrict the root system, which gives you easily handled plants and better fruit production. The pots can be stood out of doors in the summer if desired and returned to the greenhouse in early autumn.

Buy a pot-grown fig from a garden center in late autumn and pot it into a clay pot, with plenty of drainage material in the bottom. Figs are best potted in a limy medium loam (available from garden centers in bags) and, if available, some crushed brick rubble should be added to it. To start with, the pot should be only just big enough to hold the root system. Potting on to a larger pot in subsequent years can be carried out in midwinter, until the final size is reached, but only pot on when the existing pot is really full of roots. In the years when potting on is not carried out, top-dress with loam, first scraping away some of the old soil.

You can get two crops of fruit per year under glass – the first in early or mid-summer, the second in late summer or early autumn. To achieve an early crop, maintain a temperature of 50–60°F (10–15.5°C) from late winter onward. A summer temperature of about 80°F (26°C) is ideal and natural warmth should be sufficient.

Damp down the greenhouse regularly in warm conditions to provide a humid atmosphere; keep the air dry, though, when fruits are ripening. Shade is unnecessary.

The trees are rested in the winter by keeping the greenhouse only frost free and the soil mix barely moist. Increase watering and temperature in late winter.

Pruning consists of cutting back any vigorous new shoots to five leaves from their base, in summer. Aim for a succession of new shoots which will carry the fruits.

Grapes

A grape vine grown in the traditional way – a long rod (stem) trained up into the greenhouse roof – takes up a good deal of space and is not practical in the small greenhouse. Instead, try growing a grape vine in a pot.

Buy a young plant from a garden center and pot it in midwinter, in a 12in (30cm) clay pot, using a reasonably good potting soil mix. It can be kept out of doors and taken under glass in late winter, when a temperature of 50°F (10°C) should be provided. Place outdoors again after fruiting.

The main stem is trained in a spiral fashion around three 5–6ft (1.5–1.8m) bamboo canes inserted, wigwam-style, in the pot. Side shoots will be produced and will need thinning out to 12in (30cm) apart. The tips of these should then be cut out at two leaves beyond a bunch of grapes.

The main stem should be cut back annually by about half its length in winter. Cut back the side shoots, to one or two dormant buds.

The flowers must be pollinated by drawing your hand, half closed, down the truss of flowers – this distributes the pollen. Thin out the berries to give them space to grow, when they are the size of peas. Thin the center of each bunch; further thinning may also be needed as the berries grow. Use a pair of fine-pointed scissors.

Good ventilation is needed under glass and in summer a temperature of at least 55°F (13°C) is needed, but this is provided by natural warmth. A humid atmosphere is needed during high temperatures, but do not damp down the greenhouse while the vines are in flower, or when the fruits are ripening, as at these stages a dry atmosphere is needed. When the vines are in full growth water heavily and feed every two weeks.

Melons

These can be grown with or without artificial heat. Choose cultivars accordingly.

In a heated greenhouse sow seeds in early spring; in an unheated greenhouse sow in mid- to late spring. Sow two seeds, on edge, in 3in (7.5cm) pots, using soil-based mixture. Germinate in a temperature of 60°F (15.5°C). If both seeds germinate, remove the weaker. Plant out when well established in their pots. Grow in a well-manured soil bed, spacing the plants 18in (45cm) apart. A growing bag can also be used: each bag will hold two plants. The top of the root-ball must be slightly above soil

Below *Although the fig is normally a large, vigorous tree, it can be kept small if grown in pots. Two crops a year are possible under glass.*

Far right *Similarly, a grape vine can be kept small by growing a plant in a pot – a far better system for a small greenhouse than the traditional way of growing, which involves training stems up the side of a greenhouse and into the roof area.*

or soil mix level to prevent stem rot.

Tie in the main stem to horizontal wires spaced 12in (30cm) apart on one wall of the greenhouse, and even up into the roof. Pinch out the tip of the stem when the top wire is reached. Side shoots are tied in horizontally, and their tips removed just beyond the second leaf.

Keep the soil or mixture moist, and try to provide a temperature of 60–70°F (15.5–21°C) by day, and 55°F (13°C) at night. In summer, aim for 70°F (21°C) day and 60°F (15.5°C) night if possible. Shade from strong sun. Ensure moderate humidity.

Female flowers must be hand pollinated (these have a small fruit behind them). A male flower is used to pollinate a female and it should be done when the flowers are fully open. Pick off a male flower (males have just a thin stalk behind them), remove the petals, and brush the center of a female with it. Use a different male flower to pollinate each female and treat four to six females all at the same time. Only one fruit is allowed to grow on each side shoot, and when fruits start developing remove all further flowers as they appear.

Feed weekly from the time the fruits set. When the fruits start ripening in late summer or early autumn, keep the soil mix much drier, ventilate well and maintain a dry atmosphere. Fruits will need supporting with nets suspended from the roof from the time they are the size of a tennis ball.

Peaches
The best way to grow peaches under glass is as a pot-grown, dwarf, open-centered bush. The traditional way of fan training against a wall is generally too space consuming for the modern greenhouse.

Buy and plant a one- or two-year-old tree when available. Pot it into a 10in (25cm) clay pot, using a reasonably good potting soil mix, with plenty of drainage material in the bottom. Pot on in the winter until you reach a final pot size of 14in (35cm).

Initial training consists of allowing four branches to form a head. These are cut back by half in the winter after planting. All other branches, plus the main stem above them, are cut out. Routine winter pruning involves keeping the center of the tree open, so remove any crowded, crossing, or inward-growing shoots. Old fruited shoots should be cut back to new ones, which will in turn bear fruits.

The trees can, if desired, be placed out of doors for the summer, once the fruits have formed, but select a sheltered, sunny spot.

Peaches can be grown with or without artificial heat, but they do not need heat in winter. Warmth in spring prevents the flowers being damaged by frost.

Provide good ventilation in winter, but less in spring. In spring spray the trees twice a day with plain water during warm spells, and also damp down the greenhouse. The flowers must be hand pollinated. When fully open, dab the center of each in turn with a soft, artist's brush. Crowded new shoots must be thinned out but leave sufficient to fruit next year.

The fruitlets must be thinned out to leave only two or three per shoot.

In summer, maintain humid conditions by spraying and damping down, give plenty of ventilation, and feed with a fertilizer high in potash. Keep the atmosphere dry when fruits are ripening. In winter, keep the soil mix slightly moist.

Rhubarb
This can be forced in a heated greenhouse for autumn and winter use. Lift some three- or four-year-old roots in autumn once the leaves have died down. Lay them on the soil surface to become frosted for two or three weeks, then plant them in a deep box of old potting soil mix, with the buds level with the surface.

Water well in and put in a dark place. Cover them with an upturned box to exclude light, or put them under the greenhouse bench and enclose the sides with sheets of black polyethylene.

The more heat you can provide, the sooner you will be able to harvest the sticks. A temperature range of 45–60°F (7–15.5°C) is suitable. Sticks will then be ready in five to eight weeks. Do not use the roots again.

Strawberries
Pot-grown strawberries can be forced in a heated greenhouse. To obtain a worthwhile quantity, you will need at least 12 plants.

Buy young plants in mid- or late summer and pot into 5in (12.5cm) pots, using a soil-based potting mixture. Keep them out of doors until midwinter then take them into the greenhouse.

Pot on into 6in (15cm) pots. Place on a bench or shelving in really good light. Once growth starts, begin providing heat – maintain 40°F (4.5°C) to start with. If possible, increase heat gradually so that by mid-spring, when the plants will be in bloom, a temperature of 60°F (15.5°C) is being maintained.

The flowers must be hand pollinated with a soft brush – when fully open dab the center of each in turn. Feed with a liquid fertilizer every two weeks once the flowers are open, and continue until the fruits start to ripen. Keep the soil mix steadily moist from the time the fruits are starting to set.

After fruiting, plant the strawberries in the garden – do not force them again.

Far left *In the small greenhouse, the best way to grow a peach is as a small open-centered bush in a pot. Fruits are produced in late summer or early autumn and artificial heat is not needed.*

Below *If rhubarb is needed for autumn or winter use, force some roots in a heated greenhouse. Sticks can be ready for pulling in five to eight weeks, depending on the amount of heat provided.*

Above *Pots of strawberries placed in a heated greenhouse in midwinter will ripen their fruits several weeks earlier than plants outdoors.*

CHAPTER 8
A YEAR IN YOUR GREENHOUSE

The jobs to do, the flowers to enjoy and the crops to harvest all form part of the greenhouse year. Knowing what to do and exactly when to do it comes with experience, but a greenhouse calendar will help you get it right from the start.

There are so many things going on in a greenhouse throughout the year that a checklist, even for the experienced gardener, is extremely helpful, as it ensures that you do not forget to make some vital sowing or carry out an important aspect of cultivation.

The sections on crops to harvest and flowers to enjoy will help you to decide what you want to grow and enable you to have a fully stocked and productive greenhouse throughout the year. The greenhouse need not be empty in the winter, even if you do decide you cannot afford to heat it.

The information given is very general,

as the times of sowing, planting, harvesting and flowering depend on the part of the country in which you live, on weather conditions, and of course on the amount of heat you are able to provide.

Most of the plants included here need some artificial heat in the colder months, say from mid-autumn until mid-spring. Details of temperature requirements will be found under the appropriate plants in other chapters.

Plants which can be kept in a cold greenhouse (often with no artificial heat at all) over the winter, for flowers, foliage interest or crops, are as follows: alpines, dwarf hardy bulbs, daffodils, hyacinths,

tulips, crocuses, camellias, hardy annuals for spring flowering, chrysanthemums (ideally a little heat if possible to keep the air dry while in flower), ivy, beets, carrots, chicory, and some winter lettuces. The following popular fruits will survive quite happily without artificial heat in winter: figs, grapes and peaches.

There is no reason why a greenhouse or conservatory should not be used all the year round – too many amateur greenhouses are left to stand empty in winter and summer. Many plants can be grown without heat in the winter.

Midwinter

Even if the temperature is low, the days are getting longer at this time and if your greenhouse is heated, there should be plenty of plants in flower now, to boost your morale. An unheated greenhouse can be colorful, too, with a display of alpine plants, heaths and, often, camellias.

Jobs to do

Watering should be carried out very sparingly.

Ventilate whenever the weather is fine.

Sow sweet peas, African daisy *(Gerbera)*, *Begonia semperflorens* and F_1 zonal pelargoniums for summer bedding.

Sow sweet peas in individual containers

Sow carrots, green beans, lettuces, onions for later planting in the garden.

Take cuttings of heliotrope and flame nettle *(Coleus)*.

Pot new (kept dormant) peach tree, or pot on older one if required.

Pot grape vine, also kept dormant, and stand out of doors.

Move figs into larger pots if necessary or topdress with good potting soil.

Prune peach trees.

The center of a peach tree is kept open

Indian azaleas will be in full bloom

Take potted strawberry plants into the greenhouse.

Plant potato tubers in pots or growing bags.

Early potatoes should be planted now

Prune grape vine.

Cut back hard old fuchsias and re-pot into fresh potting mix.

Bring pots and bowls of hardy bulbs into the greenhouse.

Start chrysanthemum roots into growth and take cuttings as soon as shoots are long enough.

Lilies can still be potted for flowering in the greenhouse.

Remove all dead leaves and flowers from plants to prevent an attack of botrytis, or gray mold, fungus.

Plants to enjoy

Alpines, arum or zantedeschia, azaleas, dwarf bulbs, other hardy bulbs (like daffodils, hyacinths, tulips and crocuses), camellias, carnations, cyclamen, freesias, hippeastrums, ivies throughout the winter, primroses *(Primula)*, winter cherry *(Solanum capsicastrum* and *S. pseudo-capsicum)* and winter heaths *(Erica)*.

Crops to harvest

Asparagus, carrots (small stump-rooted cultivars), chicory, lettuces, radishes, rhubarb and salad onions.

Late winter

Though the ground outdoors may be frozen hard, or even under snow, you can be busy in the cool greenhouse, sowing seeds of flowers and vegetables, and putting tuberous-rooted plants, such as begonias, to sprout. Organizing the soil mixes, containers and seeds for the main sowing in spring, can be done now.

Jobs to do
Watering should be carried out very sparingly.

Ventilate whenever the weather is fine.

Make sowings of summer bedding plants such as lobelia, ageratum, petunias, antirrhinums, salvias.

Sow greenhouse pot plants – primroses

Sow African daisy for summer blooms

Cinerarias for the cool greenhouse

(Primula), winter cherry (*Solanum capsicastrum* and *S. pseudocapsicum*), African daisy (*Gerbera*).

Sow sweet peas for later planting out.

Sow tomatoes if you can provide plenty of heat, and lima beans and peas for later planting out in the garden.

Box up dormant dahlia tubers to provide cuttings (give gentle heat) and take

cuttings when available.

Take cuttings of fuchsias, and verbenas for summer bedding.

Pot rhizomes of achimenes and tubers of begonia and gloxinia.

Pot on young perpetual-flowering carnations.

Pot bulbs of amaryllis.

Sow carrots for greenhouse crops.

Increase watering and temperature for figs.

Take potted grape vine into greenhouse.

Pollinate peach flowers to ensure fruit set.

Plants to enjoy
Alpines, arum or zantedeschia, azalea, dwarf bulbs, other hardy bulbs (like daffodils, hyacinths, tulips and crocuses), camellias, carnations, cinerarias, cyclamen, freesias, amaryllis, primroses (*Primula*) and winter cherry (*Solanum capsicastrum* and *S. pseudocapsicum*).

Crops to harvest
Asparagus, carrots, lettuces and radishes.

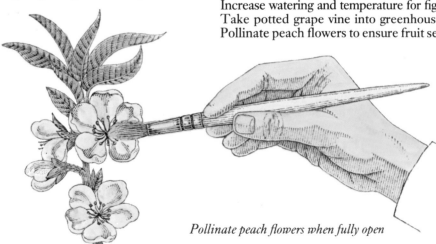

Pollinate peach flowers when fully open

Early spring

If your greenhouse is unheated, then the weather will very much determine what can be done at this time. Frosty weather is still present in the north, so be on your guard, but whatever sunlight is about will be magnified by the greenhouse glass or plastic, making conditions more favorable for the plants.

Jobs to do
Ventilate more freely in favorable weather.

Watering can now be increased.

Sow half-hardy annuals or summer-bedding plants like French and African marigolds, alyssum, annual phlox, ten-

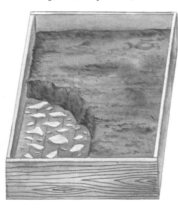

Sow seeds in well-drained seed trays

Large seeds can be sown in drills

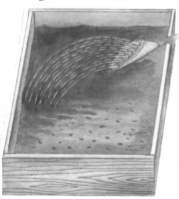

Moisten soil mix after sowing

week stocks, zinnias, asters, busy Lizzie *(Impatiens)*, mimulus, gazanias, mesembryanthemums (or Livingstone daisies), nicotiana, verbena.

Sow eggplants, tomatoes, peppers, cucumbers, beets, celery for later planting out, green beans, melons.

Sow primroses *(Primula)*, freesias, Cape primrose *(Streptocarpus)*, winter cherry *(Solanum capsicastrum* and *S. Pseudocapsicum)*.

Pinch out young fuchsias to make them branch.

Take cuttings of outdoor chrysanthemums, dahlias, heliotrope, verbena, flame nettle *(Coleus)*, perpetual-flowering carnations and many greenhouse plants.

Buy and pot up some new fuchsias.

Start old fuchsias into growth by increasing temperature and watering.

Prune the paper flower *(Bougainvillea)* and the passion flower *(Passiflora caerulea)*.

Feed autumn-sown annuals in pots.

Pot on as required young cyclamen, pelargoniums and fuchsias.

Harden off sweet peas in a cold frame ready for planting outdoors.

Pot up tubers of begonias and gloxinias.

Pot-grown daffodils make a fine spring display in a cold or cool greenhouse

Plants to enjoy
Alpines, arums or zantedeschia, azaleas, hardy annuals sown in autumn, dwarf hardy bulbs, other hardy bulbs (like daffodils, hyacinths, tulips and crocuses), camellias, carnations, cinerarias, cyclamen, freesias, amaryllis, primroses *(Primula)*, poor man's orchid *(Schizanthus)*, slipperwort *(Calceolaria)*, winter cherry *(Solanum capsicastrum* and *S. pseudocapsicum)*.

Crops to harvest
Asparagus, carrots, lettuces and radishes.

Mid-spring

With the increasing light levels, plant growth in the greenhouse will speed up. Be careful, though, as the light and warmth that encourage plants also encourage dormant greenhouse pests to become active again.

Jobs to do

Ventilation can now be considerably increased.

Shading should be used, especially for seedlings.

Watering will need to be increased.

Make sowings of half-hardy annuals or summer-bedding plants.

Sow vegetables – tomatoes, cucumbers, green beans.

Sow melons.

Sow pot plants – primroses *(Primulas)*, busy Lizzie *(Impatiens)*, cinerarias, celosia, flame nettle *(Coleus)*.

Prick out seedlings sown earlier.

Prick out seedlings into seed trays or pots

Pollinate the flowers of strawberries when fully open.

Plant tomatoes, eggplants, cucumbers, peppers, melons in heated greenhouse.

Pot on fuchsias as necessary and give them their final stopping.

Stand camellias out of doors after flowering in mild areas.

Harden off outdoor chrysanthemums in a cold frame before planting out.

Most freesias are beautifully scented

A mushroom kit can be started off now

Mushrooms can be started this month.

Take cuttings of hydrangeas.

Plant hanging baskets with suitable plants, such as trailing fuchsias, petunias, lobelia and alyssum.

Greenhouse chrysanthemums will need final potting.

Any foliage pot plants and other permanent pot plants can be potted on as necessary at this time of year.

Side shoots of grape vines will need pinching back.

Flowers of grapes will need pollinating when fully open.

Watering of cacti can be increased from now onward.

When freesias have finished flowering, the corms can be gradually dried off.

Regular feeding of all actively growing plants can commence now and should continue throughout spring and summer. Regular damping down can now be started.

Plants to enjoy

Alpines, arums or zantedeschia, hardy annuals, dwarf hardy bulbs, other hardy bulbs (like daffodils, hyacinths, tulips and crocuses), camellias, carnations, cinerarias, clivias, freesias, amaryllis, hydrangeas, primroses *(Primula)*, poor man's orchid *(Schizanthus)* and slipperwort *(Calceolaria)*.

Crops to harvest

Asparagus, carrots, green beans, lettuces and potatoes from midwinter planting.

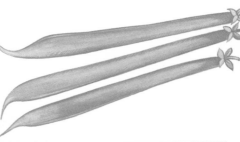

Late spring

With reasonable weather and a reasonably sheltered garden, you should be able to speed up moving some of your flower and vegetable seedlings outdoors, or harden them off before planting out. This will give you more room in the greenhouse to continue successional sowing and potting on.

Jobs to do

Water freely from now onwards.
Damp down regularly, especially in warm weather.
Give plenty of ventilation when warm.
Shade plants from strong sunshine.
Harden off in a cold frame all plants which are to be planted in the garden, including summer bedding plants.

Pot on perpetual-flowering carnations to final pots.
Sow pot plants – cineraria, slipperwort

(Calceolaria), busy Lizzie *(Impatiens)*, primroses *(Primula)*.
Make sowings of green beans.

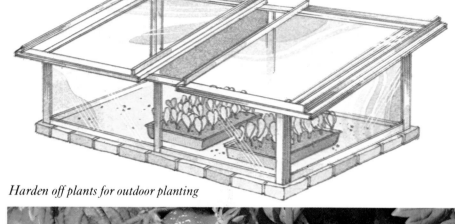

Harden off plants for outdoor planting

Plant eggplants, cucumbers, peppers, tomatoes and melons.
Mushrooms can be started, using proprietary mushroom kit.
Pollinate the flowers of grapes when fully open.
Dry off cyclamen tubers.
Cuttings can be taken of hydrangeas.

Make hydrangea cuttings from new shoots

Artificial heat can be turned off, certainly by the end of this period.
Insulation material can be removed once the heat has been turned off.

Plants to enjoy

Hardy annuals, African daisy *(Gerbera)*, bird of paradise *(Strelitzia reginae)*, carnations, clivia, fuchsias, hydrangeas, regal pelargoniums, slipperwort *(Calceolaria)* and wax flower *(Hoya carnosa)*.

Crops to harvest

Asparagus, beets, green beans, lettuces and strawberries.

Early summer

The days are at their longest now, and this is often one of the most attractive times of the year in the greenhouse and garden alike. With the advent of hot weather a real possibility, greenhouse watering and ventilation will become regular tasks.

Jobs to do

Provide plenty of ventilation.

Shade plants from strong sunshine.

Water plants freely.

Damp down regularly, especially in warm weather.

Greenhouse chrysanthemums can now be stood outdoors for the summer.

Stand hydrangeas outdoors when flowering is over, and fig and peach trees.

Spray open flowers of winter cherry *(Solanum capsicastrum* and *S. pseudocapsicum)* with water to encourage fruit set, and stand plants outdoors.

Place young cyclamen, cinerarias, young hydrangeas, primroses or primulas in a cold frame.

There is still time to sow primroses *(Primula)*, slipperwort *(Calceolaria)* and cinerarias.

Take cuttings of regal pelargoniums and fuchsias.

The earliest tomatoes may be ready

Pelargonium cuttings rooted now will provide next year's flowering plants

Thin bunches of grapes as soon as the berries reach the size of peas.

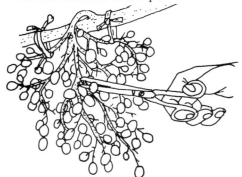

Remove male flowers of cucumbers from now onward.

Pinch out side shoots of cucumbers and melons, and also remove side shoots of tomatoes.

Pollinate flowers of peppers, tomatoes and melons and continue pollinating for as long as necessary.

Plants to enjoy

African daisy *(Gerbera)*, tuberous begonias, bird of paradise *(Strelitzia reginae)*, brunfelsia, busy Lizzie *(Impatiens)*, Cape primrose *(Strepto-*

Gloxinias need shade and high humidity

carpus), perpetual-flowering carnations, flame nettle *(Coleus)*, fuchsias, gloxinias, paper flower *(Bougainvillea)* and regal pelargoniums.

Crops to harvest

Small beets, figs, green beans, mushrooms, peppers, strawberries and tomatoes.

Midsummer

Midsummer, often the driest, hottest time of the year and though your garden may need regular watering, it is even more crucial for plants growing in the greenhouse. Damping down, to give the greenhouse a humid atmosphere, will probably be necessary, and extra feeding, to replace the nutrients washed away by frequent watering.

Jobs to do

Ventilate freely, especially in warm weather conditions.

Shade from strong sunshine.

Water freely – twice a day may be necessary.

Damp down twice a day in warm weather.

Re-pot old cyclamen tubers into fresh soil mix and start into growth.

Take cuttings of fuchsias and pelargoniums.

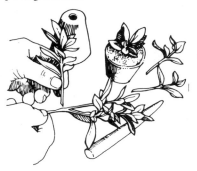

Place young perpetual-flowering carnations in cold frame for summer.

Place regal pelargoniums out of doors for a few weeks in a warm sheltered spot.

Place winter cherry (*Solanum capsicastrum* and *S. pseudocapsicum*) out of doors for the summer and spray the flowers daily with water.

Pot on any root-bound, containerized plants.

Feed greenhouse chrysanthemums and water well.

Prune fig trees – cut back new shoots.

Pot and place out of doors young strawberry plants intended for forcing.

Plants to enjoy

Achimenes, African daisies (*Gerbera*), tuberous begonias, bird of paradise (*Strelitzia reginae*), brunfelsia, busy Lizzie (*Impatiens*), cacti, Cape primrose (*Streptocarpus*), carnations, celosias, fuchsias, gloxinias, paper flower (*Bougainvillea*), passion flower (*Passiflora caerulea*) and regal pelargoniums.

Crops to harvest

Eggplants, cucumbers, figs, green beans, mushrooms, peaches, peppers and tomatoes.

Above left *Take cuttings of fuchsias. Using a dibbler, plant three or four of them into each small pot.*

Above right *Figs can be pruned, cutting back any new shoots, and harvested.*

Below left *The shrub brunfelsia flowers freely throughout the summer.*

Below right *Mushrooms will be ready for gathering. Gently twist them out rather than cutting the stalks.*

Late summer

Though the days are getting shorter, they can still be very hot, and various pests and diseases, encourged by the warmth, can be a problem in the greenhouse. Whitefly, in particular, may need dealing with, and fungal infections, especially mildew.

Jobs to do

Ventilate freely, especially in warm weather conditions.

Shade from strong sunshine.

Water freely – check twice a day for requirements.

Damp down twice a day in warm conditions.

Take cuttings of regal and zonal pelargoniums.

Sow seeds of poor man's orchid *(Schizanthus),* hardy annuals for spring flowering in pots, cyclamen.

Sow seeds of salad vegetables, including chicory and lettuces.

Cyclamen seeds can be hand spaced

Pot freesia corms and place in a cold frame.

Start to reduce watering of amaryllis to give the bulbs a rest.

Pot and place out of doors young strawberry plants intended for forcing.

Check supports for heavy-fruited plants such as melons.

Above *Cucumbers will be ready for harvesting. There is no need to wait until they become very long – small fruits are just as good.* **Right** *Cape primroses flower throughout summer and need shade and high humidity*

Plants to enjoy

African daisies *(Gerbera),* tuberous begonias, bird of paradise *(Strelitzia reginae),* brunfelsia, busy Lizzie *(Impatiens),* Cape primrose *(Streptocarpus),* carnations, celosias, Chilean bellflower *(Lapageria rosea),* fuchsias, gloxinias, paper flower *(Bougainvillea)* and passion flower *(Passiflora caerulea).*

Crops to harvest

Eggplants, cucumbers, figs, grapes, melons, mushrooms, peaches, peppers and tomatoes.

Early autumn

With the advent of cooler weather, many greenhouse plants seem to perk up, and flower more profusely than they did in the oppressive summer heat. It is a good time to clean up the greenhouse, after all the activity of spring and summer, to make it ready for the winter season.

Jobs to do

Plants will now be requiring less water.

Shading can be dispensed with.

Give less ventilation from now onwards but continue with some ventilation throughout autumn and winter.

Stop damping down the greenhouse.

Clear out summer crops as soon as harvesting has finished (tomatoes, cucumbers, etc).

Take the opportunity of a fairly empty greenhouse to thoroughly clean it out – scrub it down and sterilize. Also sterilize the ground beds.

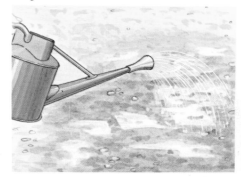

Ground beds can be sterilized with a solution of formaldehyde to kill pests

Carry out any repairs and preservation treatment.

Clean and sterilize all empty containers, such as pots and seed trays.

Start heating, and make sure the house is well insulated to conserve heat.

House and disbud chrysanthemums.

Return to the greenhouse any tender plants that have been out of doors or in a cold frame for the summer. These include cinerarias, cyclamen, freesias, hydrangeas, poor man's orchid (*Schizanthus*), primroses (*Primula*), winter cherries (*Solanum capsicastrum* and *S. pseudocapsicum*). Also return figs and peach trees to the greenhouse.

Place potted grape vines outdoors after fruiting.

Pot off seedlings of poor man's orchid (*Schizanthus*) and cyclamen.

Pot bulbs, such as daffodils, hyacinths, tulips, crocuses and dwarf hardy bulbs for a spring display when available.

Sow seeds of hardy annuals for spring flowering in pots.

Dry off tubers of begonias, gloxinias and achimenes.

Sow vegetables: carrots, lettuces, radishes in succession, and salad onions.

Buy alpine plants and pot them. Keep them in a cold frame until they are coming into flower.

Plants to enjoy

Busy Lizzie (*Impatiens*), Cape primrose (*Streptocarpus*), carnations, Chilean bellflower (*Lapageria rosea*), fuchsias, gloxinias, paper flower (*Bougainvillea*) and passion flower (*Passiflora caerulea*).

Crops to harvest

Eggplants, cucumbers, figs, grapes, melons, mushrooms, peaches, peppers, radishes and tomatoes.

Above: *Eggplant or aubergine.* **Below:** *Blooms of the blue passion flower*

Mid-autumn

Protection of frost-tender plants in the greenhouse is the prime responsibility this month. Heat will almost certainly be needed at night, and probably during the day as well, as the mild weather comes to an end. Watering will be much less frequent now, as plant growth slows down.

Jobs to do

Water plants very carefully and sparingly. Ventilate adequately according to weather conditions – keep air dry.

If not already done, move in all tender plants that have been out of doors or in a cold frame for the summer.
Start resting Cape primroses *(Strepto-carpus)* by reducing watering.
Dry off old fuchsias to rest them over the winter.
Make sowings of carrots and lettuces.
Lift and box rhubarb crowns for forcing in heated greenhouse.
Pot lily bulbs for flowering in the greenhouse next spring/early summer.

Plants to enjoy

Busy Lizzie *(Impatiens)*, carnations, Chilean bellflower *(Lapageria rosea)*, chrysanthemums and cyclamen.

Crops to harvest

Eggplants, lettuces, peppers, radishes and tomatoes. There may be a few fruits left on the summer crops.

Below left *Whenever the weather permits, open greenhouse windows and doors to allow for plenty of ventilation.*

Bottom left *Lilies can be potted up and kept out of direct light to ensure early blooms for bringing indoors or for color in the greenhouse.*

Below *Cut chrysanthemums when open.*

Late autumn

This is a quiet time of the year in the greenhouse, with very little sowing or potting on to be done. Though the air may be cold, as long as it is not frosty some ventilation will be needed. Fresh air helps to keep the plants healthy and discourages the build-up of fungal infections, such as damping off, associated with moist, stagnant air.

Jobs to do
Water plants very carefully and sparingly.
Ventilate adequately according to weather conditions. Keep air dry.
Start to bring in bulbs for forcing.
Cut down the stems of autumn-flowering chrysanthemums as soon as flowering is over and put plants in cold frame.

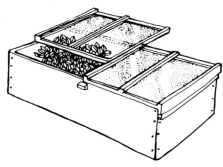

Take dwarf hardy bulbs into the greenhouse and place on the benches in good light.
Keep cacti dry from now onwards, but forest cacti (like the Christmas cactus) must not be allowed to dry out.
Take potted camellias into the greenhouse for winter and spring flowers.
Make more sowings of lettuces.
Buy a young fig tree and pot it.
Reduce watering of fig trees to rest them.
Lift and box asparagus and rhubarb crowns for forcing in a heated greenhouse.

Blanch chicory for several weeks

Plants to enjoy
Carnations, chrysanthemums, cyclamen, primroses *(Primula)* winter cherry *(Solanum capsicastrum* and *S. Pseudocapsicum).*

Crops to harvest
Carrots (stump-rooted forcing cultivars for autumn/winter use), chicory, lettuces, radishes, rhubarb and salad onions.

Below *Cacti should be kept dry from now until mid-spring, but if plants shrivel excessively during the winter a little water may be given. Keep them cool and ensure they receive maximum light.* **Bottom** *However, the forest cacti, like the popular Christmas cactus, should be watered during its growing period, keeping soil mix slightly moist.*

Early winter

A cool greenhouse can be a great help in early winter, in the bringing on of flowering plants, including forced bulbs, to decorate the house for Christmas. After their stint in a centrally heated house, the plants can be returned, together with any pot plants you may have received as gifts, to the more congenial greenhouse environment, to continue their display.

Jobs to do
Water plants very sparingly and do not splash water around.
Ventilate adequately according to weather conditions. Keep air dry.
Cut down the stems of late-flowering chrysanthemums as soon as flowering is over and put plants in cold frame.

Box up chrysanthemum roots in soil mix

Pot and keep cool bulbs for forcing.
Prune grape vines and peach trees.
Hardy annuals can be transferred from the cold frame to the greenhouse.
Sow more lettuces.

Plants to enjoy
Azaleas, bulbs such as daffodils, hyacinths, tulips and crocuses, camellias, carnations, chrysanthemums, cyclamen, freesias, amaryllis, primroses *(Primulas)*, winter cherry *(Solanum capsicastrum* and *S. pseudocapsicum)* and winter heaths *(Erica).*

Top *Cyclamen will continue flowering for many weeks.* **Above** *One can continue forcing rhubarb roots in heat*

Crops to harvest
Carrots, chicory, lettuces, radishes, rhubarb and salad onions.

CHAPTER 9
PESTS & DISEASES

Even the most well-run greenhouse is occasionally vulnerable to pest and disease problems. Being able to recognize the problem, and deal with it as quickly and effectively as possible, will keep your plants healthy and happy, and cropping and flowering well.

Pests and diseases are troublesome enough in the open garden, but under glass they are even more of a nightmare. Due to the warm, favorable greenhouse conditions, they tend to multiply very rapidly.

As far as possible, try to prevent pests and diseases building up. Maintaining clean, hygienic conditions will go a long way toward preventing troubles. Annual washing down of the greenhouse and sterilizing, using clean containers and sterilized soil mixes, removing dead and dying plant material and generally growing plants well are all important aspects of control.

Nevertheless, pests and diseases will still appear and then you must act swiftly in an effort to eliminate them.

The most popular method is to spray plants with a liquid insecticide or fungicide. Alternatively, dusts can be used. These are particularly recommended for plants which do not like their leaves wetted, for flowers, for stored plant material and for use in autumn and winter when plants and the atmosphere should be kept dry.

Pesticides can also be applied in the form of smoke. Smoke canisters, rather like fireworks, are ignited in the greenhouse, which remains closed down for several hours to trap the smoke. Sometimes it is more convenient simply to pick off pests and destroy them, or to pick off the odd leaf infected with pest or disease.

Biological control of pests is being used more and more under glass. A parasitic or predatory insect or mite is introduced into the greenhouse to destroy a particular pest. The parasitic wasp (*Encarsia formosa*) is used to control whitefly, one of the most serious pests under glass. Another major pest, red spider mite, is controlled with a predatory mite (*Phytosieulus persimilis*). These are supplied on leaves and introduced into the greenhouse at the beginning of the growing season – early to mid-spring.

Biological control should only be used when there are whitefly or red spider mites on the plants, otherwise the predators will quickly die, for they will have nothing to feed on. Pesticides must not be used in the greenhouse when biological control has been introduced.

Below left and right *Use insecticides and fungicides strictly according to the manufacturer's instructions and apply as soon as trouble is apparent.*

Common pests

1. Aphids – *greenfly or blackfly attack many plants, sucking the sap, which weakens and distorts the plants. Control – pick off badly affected leaves; malathion sprays; smokes.*

2. Caterpillars – *larvae of moths or butterflies, generally greenish, eat leaves of plants, including carnations. Control – pick off by hand; or spray plants with malathion, derris or sevin.*

3. Earwigs – *familiar insects with "pincers" at the rear. Generally eat flower petals of carnations, chrysanthemums and other plants. Control – dust or spray flowers and foliage with sevin.*

4. Eelworms – *often live inside plant tissue, microscopic. Attack many plants, including chrysanthemums and tomatoes. Severely weaken and distort growth. Control – destroy affected plants.*

5. Leaf miners – *tiny white grubs which tunnel inside leaves of chrysanthemums and cinerarias, severely weakening them. Tunnels can be clearly seen. Control – remove affected leaves; use systemic (not on food plants) or malathion sprays.*

6. Mealy bugs – *soft bugs covered in whitish powder, which attack many plants, sucking the sap and weakening growth. Control – pick off; use malathion or systemic (not on food plants) sprays.*

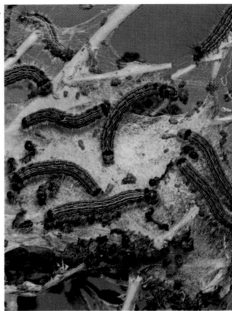

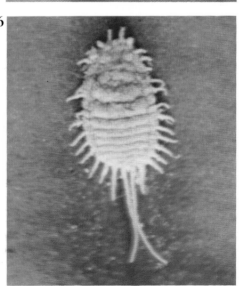

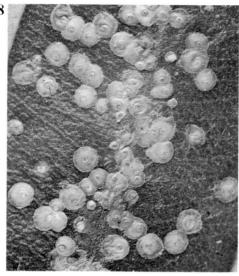

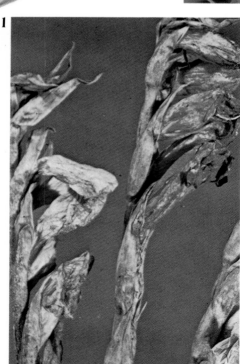

7. Red spider mites – *barely visible reddish "spiders." Suck sap of many plants, resulting in pale mottling on the leaves. Control – ideally biological; humid atmosphere discourages these pests.*

8. Scale insects – *scale-like creatures, brown, stationary. Suck sap of many plants, weakening them. Control – pick or scrape off; use malathion sprays if colonies are very large.*

9. Slugs – *these well-known creatures attack many soft plants, such as lettuces. They eat leaves, stems and fruits. Control – use slug pellets around plants.*

10. Snails – *cause same damage as slugs and controlled in the same way.*

11. Thrips – *very small brown insects, attack many plants, sucking sap, causing speckled leaves and flowers. The photograph shows damage to gladioli flowers. Control – use sprays of malathion as soon as symptoms are noticed.*

12. Whitefly – *one of the most serious pests. Tiny white flies weaken plants by sucking sap. Found on undersides of leaves. Control – insecticidal soap, spray or biological control.*

Common diseases

1. Blossom end rot – *brown or black circular patch at the "blossom end" of tomato fruits. Caused by shortage of water when young fruits are developing. Control – make sure soil never dries out completely.*

2. Botrytis – *or gray mold. Gray fungus on all parts of plants. Causes rotting. Most plants susceptible. Control – clean, hygienic conditions; ensure good ventilation; remove affected material; spray plants with benomyl fungicide.*

3. Damping off – *a seedling disease – seedlings collapse and die. Control – soil mixes and containers must be sterilized.*

4. Mildew – *leaves and shoot tips have white powdery covering. Results in distorted growth. Many plants attacked, especially lettuces and grapes. Control – spray non-food plants with benomyl; ensure good ventilation.*

5. Peach leaf curl – *leaves of peaches become curled and bright red. Also attacks nectarines. Control – in late winter spray with any approved fungicide.*

6. Potato blight – *attacks potatoes and tomatoes. Brown patches on foliage; dark-brown patches on tomato fruits, followed by rotting. Control – use zineb sprays in early summer.*

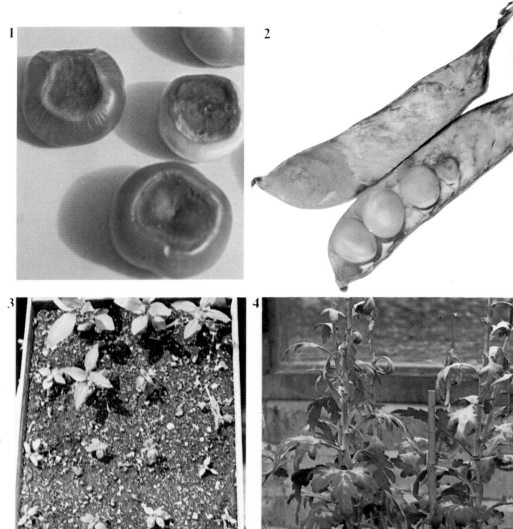

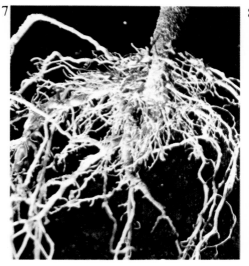

7. Root rot – *common with tomatoes. Roots rot and plant wilts. Control – generally caused by very wet soil, so avoid overwatering.*

8. Rust – *several plants attacked – chrysanthemums, carnations and pelargoniums particularly. Symptoms are brown-orange spots on leaves. Control – badly affected leaves should be picked off. Use zineb or thiram sprays.*

9. Stem rot – *susceptible plants are tomatoes, melons and cucumbers. Base of stem rots, plants collapse. Control – caused by careless watering – make sure you do not wet the base of the stems.*

10. Tomato leaf-mold – *tomatoes attacked. Brown-yellow fungus on leaves, which become distorted and weakened. Control – use sprays of thiram as soon as seen.*

11. Wilt – *another common disease of tomatoes. Plants first wilt and then collapse. Control – affected plants should be destroyed; plant only in sterilized soil; maintain correct growing conditions (see TOMATOES). The photograph shows virus spotted wilt: plants with this should also be destroyed.*

12. Viruses – *many plants attacked, including tomatoes and cucumbers. Various symptoms: leaves often streaked or mottled with yellow; stunted or distorted growth; deformed fruits or flowers. Control – affected plants must be destroyed. Destroy aphids, as they spread viruses.*

INDEX

Picture Credits

Front cover: Michael Warren

Back cover: Valerie Finnis

AGL: 20, 22(l), 23(l&tr) 24; A–Z Collection: 41, 66(br); Amateur Gardening: 58, 61(bl), 64(br); Ardea Photographic: 59(br); P. Ayers: 54, 55(tr); Paul Beatie: 10, 12, 15, 16/7; P. Becker: 68(cr), 69(tr); Steve Bicknell: 27; Pat Brindley: 57(tr), 62(tr); Michael Boys: 25(tl); Compton Aluminium Greenhouses: 1; R. J. Corbin: 25(tr), 28, 55(tl), 59(tr), 62(tl), 65(bl), 67, 68(bl), 70(tl); John Cowley: 29(bl); Eric Chrichton: 38, 60(b); Roy Day: 9; Dobies Seeds: 44; P. Dowell: 63(t); Alan Duns: 25(b); Ray Duns: 14; Valerie Finnis: 4, 60(t); Brian Furner: 2/3, 56(br); J. Grant: 69(bl); Iris Hardwick Library: 51; Grant Heilman: 47; Hovel Manufacturers: 22(r); John Hovell: 18, 19; George Hyde: 68(tr), 70(bl); ICI: 69(tl), 71(tl&tr); Elsa Megson: 63(b); Tania Midgley: 5; Ministry of Agriculture Fisheries and Food: 71(br); Murphy Chemical Co.: 70(cl,cr), 71(bl); Plant Protection Ltd: 70(br); J. Roberts: 69(cr); G. Rodway: 23(br); Shell: 70(tr); Miki Slingsby: 37; Harry Smith Horticultural Photographic Collection: 34, 43, 45, 48, 49, 50, 52, 56(tl,tr), 57(r), 59(l), 62(br), 65(br), 66(tr); Colin Watmough: 36, 39; D. Wildridge: 40; C. Williams: 68(br).